"Ross has a passion to with 'The Real Jesus.' J revelation of the Scriptures is reflected the unadulterated Word of God. *Selah* is a devotional book that epitomizes everything about the author. It is written in a way that reflects the rawness, the awe, the beauty, the anger, the vulnerability, the sorrow, the joy, and the hope of following Jesus. Every reader's heart will be lifted up to consider the truths of the Psalms and the God who wrote them. It is a devotional book that I would recommend to every person who follows Jesus. It will guide you into a deeper and more intimate relationship with Jesus Christ."

— **Tich Smith,**
Founder of the Lungisisa Indlela Village (LIV),
an orphan village in KZN, South Africa,
Co-author of *When Grace Showed Up:*
One Couple's Story of Hope and Healing among the Poor

"Ross Lester is a man who strives to live a life that reflects a heart immersed in the Scriptures. So as he takes us through the Psalms, you can see that each word has been thoroughly thought through, revealing that his approach to this poetic book is from a place of utter devotion. He allows you to witness a heart and mind that has wrestled with the Word of God and invites you to do the very same. His vulnerability, dripping from every page, will encourage you to come before the Lord in honesty, with no face mask on, declaring imperfections. Ross will then point you to God, over and over, revealing to you that no matter what you are going through or where you are in life, we are all in desperate need of a Savior, who loves us more than we could ever imagine."

— **One Mokgatle,**
Lead Pastor of Rooted Fellowship, Pretoria, South Africa

"There may be no better place in the Bible to experience the full gamut of human emotion than in the Psalms. Ross does an excellent job applying God's Word to the ups and downs of the Christian life. He points to the wonderful realities in the Psalms that show us how to honestly respond to God, while still being anchored in His goodness and wisdom. This book is highly accessible and a great devotional that will supplement your reading of the Psalms."

— Kevin Peck,
Lead pastor of The Austin Stone Community Church,
Austin, Texas

SELAH

DEVOTIONS FROM THE PSALMS

ROSS

FOR THOSE WHO STRUGGLE

LESTER

WITH DEVOTION

LUCIDBOOKS

TABLE OF CONTENTS

Acknowledgments

To the people of Bryanston Bible Church,

Thank you for allowing me to journey with you as we have sought to follow Christ together. Your love, warmth, prayers, and faith have been a tremendous blessing to me. Press on. To "Aunty Jenny," who pushed me to write this and who rested in the Psalms in the middle of the valley of the shadow of death. Thanks for the example, and the encouragement.

To Sue, Daniel, and Katie. Thank you for filling my life with so much love, grace, and joy. You are such gifts of God's glorious kindness to me. To the team at Lucid, and to the team at BBC who believed in this and made it happen. You all saw something I still don't see. Thank you for your support. My only hope and prayer is that perhaps a few people would find these meditations helpful and might begin to love the Psalms and find in them hope, joy, and peace.

Introduction

I love the Psalms. I love the rawness, the awe, the beauty, the anger, the vulnerability, the sorrow, the joy, the hope. There is nothing sterile, aloof, cool, safe, or glammed up about them, and that is what makes them useful to real people like you and me, who wrestle with real experiences of faith and doubt that exist hidden behind our "highlight reel" lives that we continually self-publish to the world on social media. Life can be hard, and confusing, and wonderful all at the same time, and we need to find honest, real, and worshipful ways of declaring the goodness of God in all of those times. The Psalms help us do just that. I hope and pray that as you spend the next one-hundred-and-fifty days or so reflecting on them, your heart will be encouraged and your faith will be strengthened, and you will grow in humility and honesty in your walk with our wonderful God.

WHAT IS THIS BOOK?

I originally wrote these reflections on the Psalms as a daily blog for our church website, and they haven't been edited all that much before we put them together in this book. They have a definite "feel" to them as a result, and it is important to note that before you continue. They are fairly impulsive and personal, as the idea of the blog series was that I would write reflections daily with a minimum amount of filter or editing. We wanted to capture some first impressions on the Psalms, and while I wanted to be accurate and respectful, I didn't want to be too precious or clinical in these meditations. It can intimidate people from daily study of the Scriptures if they only ever read very in-depth reflections from authors. It makes it seem as if one needs to have a theological degree in order to enjoy the Bible. This little book is more of a look

1

into what my devotion journal might look like than it is an exegetical study. As a result, these meditations are very limited in their ability as commentaries on the Psalms. They are reflections and not expositions, and they should be read with that in mind. You won't find information on chiastic structures, for instance, even though I know that a proper study of the Psalms would have to deal with such structural elements, and your life would be enriched from understanding them. You can find a recommended reading list for further study at the back of this book if you would like to dig a little deeper, and I would encourage you to do so.

WHY DID I WRITE THIS?

I wrote these devotionals as a pastor, intending them to be a gift to the congregation at Bryanston Bible Church in Johannesburg, South Africa. Many of the people in our church were struggling to engage with the Scriptures daily—even though they wanted to—and so I wanted to model to them what it looked like to have Scripture speak to us and to our circumstances. My deep hope was that it would give our people a small taste of what daily time in the Scriptures looks like and that it would drive them deeper into a pursuit of God's Word as the foundation of wisdom for their lives.

HOW SHOULD IT BE USED?

The best way to use this book would be as a daily devotional. It has three main elements for each of the 150 days. First is the reading. I have highlighted a couple of verses from each psalm for every day, but the reader would definitely get the most out of the meditations if they read the whole psalm for each day. Second is the short meditation I wrote as a reflection of the psalm's big idea that impacted me most. These meditations try to capture a single idea from the psalm, rather than commenting on it in its entirety. Read it slowly. Last is the prayer that follows every meditation.

Use these devotions to shape your time in the Scripture. Use them on your own, or pray together as a family or couple if you are using this book to shape your family devotions. Please don't skip over the reflection and prayer times. They are designed to last only a few minutes, but I do feel like they will add a great deal to what you learn, and how you engage with God after He has engaged with you through His Word.

I have divided this book into the same book divisions that occur in Psalms (Book 1: Psalms 1–41; Book 2: Psalms 42–72; Book 3: Psalms 73–89; Book 4: Psalms 90–106 and Book 5: Psalms 107–150). Between each book division is a "Selah" point where there is the opportunity to stop and reflect and look back on what God has been teaching you. Don't rush over those.

> The first qualification for judging any piece of workmanship from a corkscrew to a cathedral is to know what it is—what it was intended to do and how it is meant to be used.[1]
>
> C.S. Lewis

A FEW THOUGHTS ON THE PSALMS

As someone who taught English Literature at a high school for a few years, I knew the value of making sure that students understood the nature of the texts they were reading. A clear understanding of genre and context makes a significant difference in one's ability to rightly interpret a text. It is no different when it comes to Scripture, and so we should have questions about what the Psalms are to help rightly understand what the Psalms mean. Here are a few characteristics of the Psalms that may help.

---

1. C. S. Lewis, *A Preface to Paradise Lost* (Oxford: Oxford University Press, 1961).

The Psalms are poetic.

It may surprise you to know that approximately half of the Old Testament is written as poetry. This doesn't make it untrue or even allegorical, but it does change the way we approach the text. The Psalms are poetic, and the writers use poetic and literary devices all the time. They are full of imagery and symbolism, beauty and distress, hard truths and soothing graces. They are not supposed to be a science textbook, a historical collective, or even a systematic theology. These are songs and poems, and if we miss that, we miss a great deal of their beauty and power.

The Psalms are diverse.

They have different authors (David writes approximately seventy-two of them, so far as we can tell, but there are a few other authors). They are written in different times and settings (the oldest psalm is likely Psalm 90, written in 1450 B.C. and the youngest psalms are "post-exilic," making them likely to be written no earlier than 500 B.C.). And they are written in different styles with different purposes. This can make the Psalms quite disjointed to read, but it is also really encouraging, as it shows us how God values diversity and creativity as an impulse and valuable expression of worship. If one were to look for an overwhelming theme in the Psalms, one would probably have to be content with the name itself. Psalms means "book of praises," and the Psalms are full of praises to God from different people, at different times, in different circumstances—but all praising God. This, too, is a lesson to us, as God is always worthy of praise even when circumstances are tough and God seems distant. Even though there are over seventy psalms of lament, even those are turned to praise.

The Psalms are often prophetic.

Many of the psalms seem to suggest that they are speaking about someone or something that has not yet come. The blessed man in Psalm 1 is an example. It seems to function not only to call the hearers to a new way of living, but also to point toward one who would ultimately fulfill that new way. Psalm 22 is also a great example of a prophetic psalm.

> My God, my God, why have you forsaken me?
> Why are you so far from saving me, from the words of
> my groaning?

David was clearly speaking about himself, but he was also prophetically pointing toward one greater than David. He was drawing our minds and hearts toward the fact that the Son of David would be the new and better David who would also cry out those same words.

The Psalms are repetitive.

There are so many repeat ideas and themes in the Psalms that they can give you a real sense of déjà vu as you read through them. For instance, there are dozens of psalms of lament. They are different types of laments to be sure, but that is still a lot of lamenting in one volume of songs. Because of that, you will come across a number of repeated ideas in this book. I wrestled through this as I edited these, as the same ideas kept coming up, but I am at peace that God clearly wants to communicate some stuff to us that we obviously need lots of reminding about.

The Psalms are inspired.

The Holy Spirit is the ultimate author of the Psalms. It is very important for us to remember this as we engage with them, and it should significantly alter our posture as we read them. If we disagree with the Psalms, we are wrong and we need to adjust accordingly. Please don't come to Psalms as a judge who gets to weigh their worth, but rather come as a worshipper who gets to be weighed by the Scriptures, willing to adjust course when wisdom greater than our own is presented to us.

With all that in mind, let's get started. Read one a day. Read them on your own, or with others. Just read them and enjoy God.

BOOK ONE
(1 – 41)

It is not that every sentiment expressed by a psalmist is admirable, but that in praying the Psalms, we confront ourselves as we really are. The Psalms are a reality check to keep prayer from becoming sentimental, superficial, or detached from the real world.

— *Richard H. Schmidt*

The psalms train us in honest prayer.

— *Eugene Peterson*

Psalm 1

The Pursuit of Happiness Runs into Oncoming Traffic

Reading:

Take time to read the entire psalm, and then come back to read the following verses again.

> *¹ Blessed is the man*
> > *who walks not in the counsel of the wicked,*
> *nor stands in the way of sinners,*
> > *nor sits in the seat of scoffers;*
> *² but his delight is in the law of the LORD,*
> > *and on his law he meditates day and night.*
> > > *Psalm 1:1–2*

Reflection:

When my wife Sue and I lived in Seattle, Washington, one of our favorite sunny day activities was to head down to a place called the Ballard Locks. There, we would watch the boats come and go from Lake Union to the Puget Sound, but the best thing about the Locks is watching the salmon swim up the salmon ladder to return to their spawning ground. It is a remarkable thing to see. They strive and strain against a fierce and unending flow of water. It would be much easier for them to swim with the current, but it is imprinted in them to swim the other way.

The Psalms start by describing a new and different kind of person. A righteous one, a blessed one, and one who sticks out from the crowd. So much so that many commentators and scholars suggest that this psalm can be talking only about Jesus. Even if it is, it is still describing someone that followers of Christ should strive to be like.

How exactly is this man different? He refuses to follow the path of least resistance and give in to the thinking of the day. He pursues a different path, one that will seem foolish to those looking in on his life, but one that will ultimately lead to blessing, or happiness or contentment, as the word can equally be translated.

This was always supposed to be the path of the people of God. Not a well-worn highway, but a narrow and difficult track. Jesus spoke of it in his Sermon on the Mount, where he described a different kind of person, living in a new kind of Kingdom.

Blessed are the poor in spirit, those who mourn and those who are meek. Blessed are those who hunger and thirst not for stuff, but for righteousness. Blessed are the merciful, the pure in heart, the peacemakers, and those who are persecuted (Matt. 5). Popular culture isn't going to sell you any of those values as a key to contentment. The Kingdom, it seems, is upside down, or back to front, or for those prepared to swim upstream. Citizens of this Kingdom were always supposed to have been renegades and rebels, people who won't buy what society is selling. Why have we become so mainstream?

So, there are a couple of questions for us today.

What are the areas in our lives where God would ask us to repent of the fact that we have gone with the flow? Where have we followed a path of least resistance, leading to massive compromise in order to keep going? Our money? Our relationships? Our attitudes to other races or people groups? Our conversations? Our family lives? Our approach to work? What are the areas of our lives where God is asking us to live in radical obedience by actively opposing the messages of our culture, and heading in the opposite direction? Where is it that we need to take ground by swimming against the current?

I pray that as we repent and ask God to show us these areas, we will have the courage and the conviction to do what it takes to follow Him and the ways of this new kind of Kingdom.

The pursuit of joy and contentment, it would seem, lies in the journey upstream. Get swimming.

Prayer:

Dear Lord, forgive us for the ways that we have lived to please the world more than we lived to please you. Forgive us for where we have forsaken the call to live with bravery in bold rebellion against the status quo. Empower us by your Spirit to live lives that stick out, to live the kind of lives that are blessed by you and seem strange to the world. Thank you for the example your Son set, and the grace He gives to us. It is in His name we pray, amen.

Psalm 2

No Safe Jesus

Reading:

Take time to read the entire psalm, and then come back to read the following verses again.

> ⁶ *"As for me, I have set my King*
> *on Zion, my holy hill."*
> ⁷ *I will tell of the decree:*
> *The LORD said to me, "You are my Son;*
> *today I have begotten you.*
> ⁸ *Ask of me, and I will make the nations your heritage,*
> *and the ends of the earth your possession.*
> ⁹ *You shall break them with a rod of iron*
> *and dash them in pieces like a potter's vessel."*
> *Psalm 2:6–9*

Reflection:

Sometimes, it can feel like the world is going to hell in a handbasket. In South Africa where I live, we seem to have become all too accustomed to receiving and spreading bad news about what can appear to be at times a rapidly decaying society. The only good thing about this is that it has opened our eyes as a people to the futility of hope in purely political solutions to the world's problems, but it has also made us into hard and sometimes despondent people.

In Psalm 2, David got a glimpse into the future after looking at what was then a fairly bleak present scenario, and saw that there was a King coming who would be different from every other ruler. He would be the anointed Son of the Most High, and He would rule and reign with justice and power. He would rule with an iron scepter as a true and just King forever. This is a beautiful portrait of King Jesus a long time before He materialized in human form.

The problem, though, is that most of us don't have this picture of Jesus. The Jesus we picture is Scandinavian and manicured. He is always aloof and kind of cheery about everything, and He has a pithy, helpful, moralistic saying for every occasion, like a walking Northern European fortune cookie.

David's picture of Jesus wasn't safe or comfortable. It's the picture of the true, resurrected Christ who overcame evil in humility and gentleness but now rules and reigns over everything as a victorious warrior. He already has his iron scepter (Rev. 19:15), and one day he is returning to call all who are his to himself forever. The world isn't going to hell in a handbasket: it will have just leadership one day. We can't wait for that day.

I love how C. S. Lewis chose to depict Jesus in his *Chronicles of Narnia*. Aslan is a massive and powerful lion who is loving and caring toward the children, but who strikes deep fear into the hearts of his enemies. In *The Lion, The Witch and The Wardrobe*, Lucy asked Mr. Beaver about this mythical Aslan creature she has heard about. She was pretty scared to meet him, so she asked if he was safe.

> "Safe?" said Mr. Beaver… "Who said anything about safe? 'Course he isn't safe. But he's good. He's the King, I tell you."[2]

---

2. C. S. Lewis, *The Chronicles of Narnia: The Lion, the Witch and the Wardrobe* (New York: HarperCollins, 2001), 89.

Many of us need to get rid of our safe view of Jesus—the Bible doesn't describe Him that way. Reject Him outright as deplorable, or receive Him totally as Lord and King, but please don't try to accommodate Him or, heaven forbid, domesticate Him. There is no such thing as a tame lion.

This picture of Jesus brings hope to those of us who are suffering. Jesus can make it right one day, and He will. It also raises some questions for all of us who claim to follow Jesus. If He is really Lord of all, then what are the areas where we are yet to yield lordship to Him? We either bow our knee today, or we will bow our knee on that day when He returns, but we will bow. Do it now.

Prayer:

Dear Lord, forgive us for the times when we take our eyes off of you and allow ourselves to become intimidated and fearful due to the state of our world. Father, give us an accurate picture of your Son Jesus. Help us see Him as He truly is, and let that picture give us courage to live as people of justice and as citizens of your Kingdom on earth. It is in Jesus's mighty name that we pray, amen.

Psalm 3

Dear God, Please Punch That Guy in the Mouth

Reading:

Take time to read the entire psalm, and then come back and read the following verse again.

> *Arise, O LORD!*
> *Save me, O my God!*
> *For you strike all my enemies on the cheek;*
> *you break the teeth of the wicked.*
> *Psalm 3:7*

Reflection:

I haven't heard this part of Psalm 3 taught on all that much. I certainly haven't heard it quoted in a prayer meeting or a worship event. So, I got to thinking—why is Psalm 3 even in the Bible? Isn't it offensive to pray to God for Him to physically assault someone? Maybe, it's in there because God wants to show us He is okay with it being in there.

In our largely western view of a very much Middle-Eastern religious tradition, we've made our prayer and worship responses into a mono-emotional event. We like to wrap things up in a nice bow and make sure that it resolves. There is very little space left for tension and angst. There is a water-tight doctrinal argument for everything under the heavens, and that should always satisfy us. Or should it?

In this psalm, David was at a major low. His son, Absalom, had stolen his kingdom from him and was pursuing him in order to kill him. David was full of angst, anger, doubt, anxiety, and a desire for revenge, all mixed up with the fact that he still loved his son. God let him pray that way, and then let that be put into the Bible for all of us to see. It would seem that maybe there is space for some tension and raw humanity in our worship. Maybe there is space for struggle in our prayer. God, it seems, is big enough and secure enough in Himself to allow us space to respectfully rant every now and then. The Bible seems to suggest that we don't always need to be "fine" or "okay." It's no good to stay mad, but it seems to be okay to get mad now and then.

So, what are you really feeling beneath your "churchy," "I'm fine" exterior? Do you have doubts, struggles, fears? Why not take them to God? I think you will find Him loving and compassionate, and like David in Psalm 3, you may feel released enough to sleep easy and not fear as a result.

Prayer:

Our Father, we confess that there are many things in our lives and in this world that confuse and even anger us. We know without a doubt that you remain in control, and we believe you are working all things for our good and your glory. But on some days, our circumstances can get the better of us. Teach us, Lord, to be more open and honest with you and with others, and increase our faith so that we trust you and live without fear. In Jesus's mighty name we pray, amen.

Psalm 4

The Key to a Good Night's Sleep

Reading:

Take time to read the entire psalm, and then come back and read the following verse again.

> *In peace I will both lie down and sleep;*
> *for you alone, O LORD, make me dwell in safety.*
> *Psalm 4:8*

Reflection:

Psalm 3 and Psalm 4 are said to be a pair intended to go together. They function as bookends for a day. Psalm 3 is a psalm for the morning, which is probably why it is so angry, and Psalm 4 is a song for the evening—a lullaby, if you like—a soothing song to hum along to before you fall asleep.

Do you ever struggle to sleep? The key to a good night's sleep, according to David, is to know that what God thinks about your right standing before Him is way more important than what you or others believe about it. In verse 1 of the psalm, David uses a name for God that isn't used anywhere else in Scripture. He calls him, "God of my righteousness." Now, because it is such a unique term in the Scriptures, there is a lot of argument about how best to express it. C. H. Spurgeon was fascinated by the term, and he explained it this way:

> It means, Thou art the author, the witness, the maintainer, the judge, and the rewarder of my righteousness; to thee I appeal from the calumnies and harsh judgments of men. Herein is wisdom, let us imitate it and always take our suit, not to the petty courts of human opinion, but into the superior court, the King's Bench of heaven.[3]

As David was being pursued by forces led by his son Absalom, he was having a lot of accusations thrown at him. They must have kept him up at night. "You are a sham, David. You've been a lousy king. Remember what you did with Bathsheba? Even your own son hates you." I reckon that a lot of us have voices of accusation that keep us up at night. I don't know what they sound like to you, but I certainly experience them at times in my life.

Scripture says, though, that I am "in Christ" and have a new identity that comes from Him (2 Cor. 5:17), and as a result I am free from accusation (Col. 1:22) and condemnation (Rom. 8:1). God Himself gets to make the call on my righteousness, and because the work of winning that righteousness is already completed by Jesus, it can't be taken away from me, or undone through my own failings.

Now that's reason to sleep easy.

Prayer:

Heavenly Father, forgive me for the times I base my value and worth more on what others think about me and less on the righteousness your Son accomplished for me. Teach me what it means to walk in that righteousness, and free me to sleep easy knowing you are the God of my righteousness.

---

3. C. H. Spurgeon, *The Treasury of David, Volume 1* (Bellingham, WA: Logos Research Systems, 2009), 34.

Psalm 5

Run Out of Things to Say in Prayer? Try Groaning.

Reading:

Take time to read the entire psalm, and then come back to read the following verses again.

> ¹ *Give ear to my words, O LORD;*
> *consider my groaning.*
> ² *Give attention to the sound of my cry,*
> *my King and my God,*
> *for to you do I pray.*
> *Psalm 5:1–2*

Reflection:

I get to pray with people a lot. It's part of my job, and it is an immense privilege whenever I get opportunity. I have prayed at hundreds of tables laden under feasts, and I have prayed with the homeless who had no idea where the next meal was coming from. I have prayed in maternity wards giving thanks to God for a future full of possibilities, and I have prayed in ICU wards while the doctors have turned off machines. I have prayed at weddings, with families whose eyes were moist with joy, and I have prayed at funerals, with families whose cheeks were stained with sorrow.

Sometimes, these prayers came easy, and I knew exactly what to say, but sometimes they were tough, and I ran on very little in terms of inspiration. Often, I left the event and only then felt truly free to express myself to God, not having to worry about the impact of my words on others, but free to speak my mind to my heavenly Father. Sometimes, it was only when I ran out of words that true communication between me and God took place. I have laughed until it hurt. I have shouted at the sky. I have groaned out loud, wept uncontrollably, banged on my steering wheel, and even sung at the top of my voice. Sometimes, I have done all of these in one day.

David says that this is okay. In his anguish, he doesn't need to have words. God hears his groans, and pays attention to his cries. His prayer doesn't need to be understandable—it just needs to be true.

As Christians, we have made prayer, and especially corporate prayer, into a sometimes weird parade of showing off theological chops. We remind God of what He said in the Bible; we agree a lot out loud because it makes us sound like we are paying attention; we know just when to squeeze the hand of the person standing next to us in that space between "in Jesus's name" and "amen." But all of this posturing can leave a lot of people feeling intimidated by prayer. "I can't pray like that guy, so I will just let him pray for me."

Don't have words to express how you are feeling? How about a shout? How about a groan? How about a laugh? All of those can be prayer.

It seems to me that sometimes when we run out of things to say, we get to the place where we make the most sense.

> Likewise the Spirit helps us in our weakness. For we do not know what to pray for as we ought, but the Spirit himself intercedes for us with groanings too deep for words.
>
> Romans 8:26

Prayer:

This prayer is up to you today. Be honest and open. Take your time.

Psalm 6

This Day...and THAT Day

Reading:

Take time to read the entire psalm, and then come back to read the following verses again.

> ⁴ *Turn, O* L<small>ORD</small>, *deliver my life;*
> *save me for the sake of your steadfast love.*
> ⁵ *For in death there is no remembrance of you;*
> *in Sheol who will give you praise?*
> *Psalm 6:4–5*

Reflection:

Psalm 6 is the first in a series of what is known as the Penitential Psalms. They are songs written about the sorrow of sin and the deep sadness that comes from regret. David was pleading with the Lord to not punish him for his sin and rebellion. I imagine it as written in a minor key, with a 6/8 groove bumbling along beneath it. Think Radiohead meets Johnny Cash. It's that sad, and it should be because sin is a big deal.

The feeling of separation from God brings a desperation and an urgency to David that leads him to do a few things. It leads him to pray, something that many of us stay away from when we sin. It leads him to tears (enough of them, I might add, to ruin his mattress), displaying a sorrow and contrition over sin that is humbling and exemplary. It leads him also to consider the brevity of life. David asked God to forgive him immediately, because he knew he had no guarantee there would be a tomorrow. David knew that cemeteries are silent places. The dead don't have opportunity to cry out any more.

Martin Luther apparently said that there were only two days on his calendar: this day and that day. What he meant was that we all have "that day" ahead of us. That day when our hearts will stop beating; that day when our families and friends will get the news we are gone. That day…when we will meet our Maker.

The knowledge of the certainty of that day should dramatically alter the way we live today. The problem is that most of us don't consider that day enough, and so we allow our todays to blur into each other, in the continual hope that one day we will put ourselves right with God.

Don't wait. Do it now.

If you feel like you drifted from God as a result of sin, don't hesitate a moment more. Like David, remember that God, in Christ, has unfailing love for you. Nothing is too much for Him to put right. Ask Him today.

Prayer:

Gracious and merciful Father. My days are like grass before you and I know that they will pass faster than I anticipate. Forgive me for the things I have done that put a distance between us. I deeply desire the power of your Spirit in my life now so that I might make the most of the days that I have. Thank you for your mercy displayed through your precious Son. It is in His name we pray, amen.

Psalm 7

Wake Up, God

Reading:

Take time to read the entire psalm, and then come back to read the following verses again.

> *⁶ Arise, O Lord, in your anger;*
> *lift yourself up against the fury of my enemies;*
> *awake for me; you have appointed a judgment.*
> *⁷ Let the assembly of the peoples be gathered about you;*
> *over it return on high.*
> *⁸ The Lord judges the peoples.*
> *Psalm 7:6–8a*

Reflection:

"Will you fix this?" "When?" Those were my questions to God, asked through tears, as I parked my car on the pavement. I had just listened to a news report on the radio that spoke of the gang rape of a mentally challenged teenage girl. The torture had been recorded on a cell phone camera and was being virally distributed in the country I call home. I longed for vengeance. I was desperate for justice. But nothing came. Arrests were made; bail was granted—the girl has to live on with the horror. The men will probably go to prison, but it doesn't feel like justice.

What is God doing in the world? Is He doing anything at all about injustice? Many of you might wonder if it is appropriate to ask such questions. David went a step further. He said that it felt like God may have nodded off. He cried out to Him to wake up and do something in the face of fierce injustice and wickedness. Now, David knew as well as I do that God never sleeps. What he was expressing is that sometimes His silence feels to us like He is sleeping. It feels like He isn't in control.

> Oh, let the evil of the wicked come to an end,
>   and may you establish the righteous—
> you who test the minds and hearts,
>   O righteous God!
>   Psalm 7:9

David dreamed of the day when God would rule and reign in a perfect theocracy. We all know that governments can't fix the problem. Democracy is a truly wonderful thing and by far the most just of human systems. But it can't fix the human condition, and the wickedness that seems to dwell in us, but one day it will all be fixed. Along with David, I long for that day. I long for a new heaven, and a new earth. I can't wait for a new me, and a new you. A trustworthy King, and a city that will endure forever.

In the meantime, it is left to the church to bring glimpses of that new Kingdom to earth. As Jesus taught us to pray, "Thy kingdom come. Thy will be done on earth as it is in heaven" (Matt. 6:10).

But even as I commit to that mission today again, I can't help feeling that it is ingrained in my DNA to long for another home. I want God to step in and make it right. Come on, Lord! We wait for you.

Prayer:

Father, forgive me for the faithlessness that some days leads me to believe you have vacated your post as sovereign Lord who reigns with mercy and justice. Give me eyes to see where you are at work in the world. Teach me to be someone who advances your Kingdom on earth, and hasten the day when the world will once again be justly run by you. It is in Jesus's mighty name we pray, amen.

Psalm 8

Just Sing!

Reading:

Take time to read the entire psalm, and then come back to read the
following verses.

> ¹ O LORD, our Lord,
>   how majestic is your name in all the earth!
>   You have set your glory above the heavens.
> ² Out of the mouth of babies and infants,
>   you have established strength because of your foes,
>   to still the enemy and the avenger.
> ³ When I look at your heavens, the work of your fingers,
>   the moon and the stars, which you have set in place,
> ⁴ what is man that you are mindful of him,
>   and the son of man that you care for him?
>   *Psalm 8:1–4*

Reflection:

Psalm 8 is one of my favorite psalms. It speaks of how the songs of little
children leave the enemies of God silent. When kids sing about God
and His goodness, the devil is like, "I got nothing." Why do you think

this is the case? What is it about praise from the mouths of children that God can use as a weapon, and what can we emulate from the way that they praise God so that we too can silence the enemy of God?

Kids are unrestrained. I love singing with my son Daniel, because he is too young to get embarrassed and belts out tunes and pulls dance moves without the fear of rejection. We have great dance parties in our house. He will lose that freedom at some point, and I think that will be a sad day. When I watch the kids singing, praying, and praising God at our Next Generation gatherings at our church, my heart leaps, and I think the devil flees. They have a passion and a fervor that is very powerful. How can you be more passionate and zealous in your praise of God?

Kids are quick to trust. They take us at our word, which is scary, and they take God at His Word, which is wonderful. Faith and trust are huge themes in the Scriptures. They please God, and they make the enemy of God retreat. In some way, the entire canon of Scripture can be summarized in two words,

"Trust me."

Kids teach us what real trust looks like. How can you trust God in a more childlike way?

Kids are honest. They are able to own up to failings quickly, and they are able to put failures behind them equally quickly. Their whole bodies tell us how they are feeling. Lying, it seems, is a skill that grows with age. How can you be more open and honest in your praise of God?

Followers of Christ aren't called to be childish, but Jesus Himself called us to be childlike. Sing like a kid. The devil hates that.

Prayer:

Dear Father, when I think of the stars and the moon and your handiwork in the heavens, I am moved by the fact that you are mindful of me. Teach me to express this in unrestrained praise, trust, and thanks. In Jesus's wonderful name we pray, amen.

Psalm 9

Grateful Is Glad

Reading:

Take time to read the entire psalm, and then come back to read the following verses again.

> [1] *I will give thanks to the L*ORD *with my whole heart;*
>   *I will recount all of your wonderful deeds.*
> [2] *I will be glad and exult in you;*
>   *I will sing praise to your name, O Most High.*
>   *Psalm 9:1–2*

Reflection:

It has been said that perhaps I have something of a "glass half empty" disposition. The truth is that I really want to be an optimist, but at times I feel like I have lived too long to be able to do it with a clear conscience. This can be really inhibiting to a spiritual life, though, especially as the Bible talks a lot about joy, and praise and gladness. If you are like me, it can sometimes be difficult to feel joyful or glad or prone to praise. If your current circumstances are difficult because of suffering of some sort, it is even tougher, and as a result, large parts of the Bible can seem annoying, if we're honest, because we don't feel like doing what it calls us to do.

"Sing praise to His name? Not today, thanks. I don't feel like doing that. Things aren't really going my way."

I have come to realize that this ungrateful view of the world lies at the root of most of our unhappiness. A continual and permanent dissatisfaction isn't good for the heart. We can render ourselves unable to believe the best about the future when we don't have an accurate view of how things have gone in the past. This ruins our ability to be joyful in the present as well.

As we enter Psalm 9, David's situation hadn't changed. He was still overwhelmed by his enemies. His pure emotions hadn't changed, either. The rest of the psalm is going to continue to be a lament and a plea. But there is a definite change in tone. He decided to praise; he decided to believe. He looked back at God's faithfulness toward him, and his heart exploded with praise, gladness, and rejoicing.

We tend to think that a change in our external circumstances will eventually lead to joy. David didn't wait—he made a choice. "I will praise you, and with all my heart. I won't hold back. I will tell everyone I can about how good you are and the incredible things you have done."

Here is my advice to you. If you find yourself stuck in pessimism or ever so slightly addicted to melancholy, look back on what God has done and who He is. Then praise, regardless of what you are currently facing. This isn't a pretense or a denial of what we are going through, but it is a pursuit of joy in the midst of our experience that requires a shift.

When I consider what Christ has done for me, whatever I am facing looks small. Every follower of Christ has much to be thankful for. He has already transferred you from the kingdom of darkness to the Kingdom of the Son (Col. 1:13). He has already displayed His love for you (John 3:16; 15:13). He has given you a new name (Rev. 3:12–13). He has given you an inheritance no one can take from you (Eph. 1:11). He has already defeated your enemy and is currently leading the church in a victory procession (Col. 2:15).

The news is good. Rejoice.

> Rejoice in the LORD always; again I will say, rejoice. Let your reasonableness be known to everyone. The LORD is at hand; do not be anxious about anything, but in everything by prayer and supplication with thanksgiving let your requests be made known to God. And the peace of God, which surpasses all understanding, will guard your hearts and your minds in Christ Jesus.
>
> Finally, brothers, whatever is true, whatever is honorable, whatever is just, whatever is pure, whatever is lovely, whatever is commendable, if there is any excellence, if there is anything worthy of praise, think about these things. What you have learned and received and heard and seen in me—practice these things, and the God of peace will be with you.
>
> Philippians 4:4–9

Prayer:

Father God, you have been faithful and kind and merciful toward me and I will praise and give you thanks for that. Forgive me for when I fail to see that. Teach me what it means to rejoice in you always. In Jesus's mighty name, amen.

Psalm 10

Vote Jesus

Reading:

Read the entire psalm, and then take time to come back and read the following verses.

> ^{17} *O LORD, you hear the desire of the afflicted;*
>   *you will strengthen their heart; you will incline your ear*
> ^{18} *to do justice to the fatherless and the oppressed,*
>   *so that man who is of the earth may strike terror no more.*
>
> *Psalm 10:17–18*

Reflection:

Some time ago I had the real privilege of going away to the African bushveld with some family and friends. We sat around a roaring log fire at night and spoke about what South Africans speak about on such occasions: politics. I really would have preferred to speak about rhinos and elephants and cheetahs, but we didn't. I kept quiet for most of the conversation and just listened as issue after issue arose about how people around me felt that our leaders in government were failing the people. Someone pointed out rather astutely that South Africa wasn't alone in all of this, that pretty much every leadership in the world was struggling to lead their nation well and that the poor and oppressed around the world paid the price for the leadership struggle. Eventually the group decided to consult the sage, wise, silent, bearded pastor in the corner (that's me, just for clarity's sake). What did I think? Who did I have hope in? My response—I have read the Bible, and I don't believe in politicians. I know they exist. I just don't believe they hold the hope of the world in their hands.

I am all for Christians in politics, and all for Christians having a social influence and meaningful opinion. I just don't believe that politicians will save us. My hope isn't in them. Their track record isn't all that good.

In Psalm 10, David continued with his lament from Psalm 9. He was furious that God would continue to allow rulers of this world to oppress, to steal from, and to victimize those who couldn't defend themselves. David would have been very vocal at our gathering if he could have attended. I wish he could have, as I bet he made a brilliant dinner guest. But David refused to stop in the hopeless; rather, he believed that wrongs would be made right, and he gained courage and strength from that. He knew that there was another leader that defends the fatherless, One who stands up for those who have no one to speak for them.

This leader doesn't campaign, and He doesn't need your funds, or even your vote. My hope is in Him. That may sound naïve and even escapist, but I tell you what—I was able to rock back in my chair next to that fire, and sip on a wonderful Cabernet Sauvignon, and look at the incredible stars in the African sky and smile. When my bemused family asked me what I was smiling about, I could simply say, as David concluded, "It's all gonna be okay…one day."

Prayer:

Heavenly Father, sometimes when I look around at the world I can get discouraged by the things I see. Give me the eyes of faith like David had to be able to trust you for the way you are working in the world. Come quickly, Lord Jesus.

Psalm 11

Running to a Standstill

Reading:

Read the entire psalm, and then come back to read the following verse.

> *In the* LORD *I take refuge.*
> *How then can you say to my soul,*
> *"Flee like a bird to your mountain."*
> *Psalm 11:1*

Reflection:

Reading this far in the Psalms, you will have detected that they are a really honest collection of thoughts on God, life, faith, politics, suffering, joy, and pretty much everything else. I love that there is space in the Scriptures for so much honesty, and even the feeling of human subjectivity and reflection. It's part of the reason that I trust the Bible so much.

In Psalm 11, we travel back in time a little bit, to when David was still stationed in King Saul's court. His boss, friend, and mentor, Saul, was starting to become a little, let's call it, "unstable," and David's life was seriously at risk. David's friends encouraged him to flee from danger like a timid little bird, but David refused, declaring with faith that he wouldn't flee, but would instead take refuge in the nature and goodness of God. It is as if David were saying, "All I have is the truth of who God is, and that's enough," Incidentally, it wasn't always enough for David, who flees in the end. But that gives me a strange hope, as even this man who is so esteemed in the Scripture, and so loved by God, has moments of faithlessness and fear.

This psalm, though, reminded me of Peter's response to Jesus in John 6. Jesus had been saying some pretty tough stuff, and was ensuring that His followers knew He was clearly claiming to be God, and not just a good teacher. He was also telling them that they would suffer as He would suffer. Life wasn't going to be easy. This teaching was too difficult for many to accept, and so many turned away. When Jesus asked Peter what he thought, he said, "Lord, to whom shall we go? You have the words of eternal life, and we have believed, and have come to know, that you are the Holy One of God" (John 6:68–69).

There are going to be many seasons of doubt in your life. There will be times of tremendous trial, and eras of strong temptation. Will you run away in fear to whatever feels comfortable, or will you, like Peter and David, be able to stand knowing that who God is, is enough?

We have so many daily choices between faith and fear.

So many temptations to choose comfort over God.

So many opportunities to turn away.

To whom shall you go?

"In the Lord, I take refuge."

Prayer:

Father God, I have no one else to turn to but you. I confess that there are many days that your work in the world and in my life doesn't make sense, but I know that you are faithful and true. Teach me to trust you more. Teach me to take refuge against the storms of life in you. In your Son's beautiful name I pray, amen.

Psalm 12

The Church Isn't Supposed to be Okay

Reading:

Take time to read the entire psalm, and then come back to read the following verse.

> *Save, O Lord, for the godly one is gone;*
> *for the faithful have vanished from among the children of man.*
> *Psalm 12:1*

Reflection:

There has been a definite theme and consistent tone to the psalms we have studied so far. They have been laments: songs about unhappiness, despair, dissatisfaction with the world, and sometimes even with the way God works in it. Psalm 12 continues the theme, so if you were waiting for the series to get a little happier, you are going to need to wait a little longer. But they will pick up, I promise.

What I love about Psalm 12 is that it isn't individualistic. It is supposed to be what theologians call a community lament. It is a song that people like to sing together. Unfortunately, it isn't a very happy song. This isn't a pop tune.

Now, I love that this sort of expression exists in Scripture, because I am a generation "X-er" who grew up with grunge music as the community songs of privileged and yet disgruntled youth. The screams and wails of Nirvana, Pearl Jam, Soundgarden, and The Stone Temple Pilots shaped my young experience, and gave voice to much of what I was feeling. They sang about the fact that the world wasn't all right. Their response was to disconnect from it and see who could be the most miserable, but when they looked at the world, they knew it was in trouble. I still have days when these bands are all I want to listen to, even though the albums are over twenty years old now.

As I page through Scripture, I can't help thinking that we aren't as dissatisfied with the state of the world as we should be. Don't get me wrong, the Bible calls for us to live at peace as far as we can, and to have contentment with what we have, but the people of God are supposed to be people who aren't okay with the trajectory of the world. We are supposed to cry out against injustice, corruption, wickedness, and deceit. We are also supposed to point to the other way of the Kingdom of Heaven. Why have we become so okay with all we see around us? I am not proposing that we join the cultural isolationists, shouting and throwing stones at popular politics. I mean we are supposed to be a different kind of people providing an alternative to the big machine of popular thinking. There is another way to live. There is God's way.

I came across a great quote from R. Wolcombe, one of the commentators on this psalm. He says:

> Consider our markets, our fairs, our private contracts
> and bargains, our shops, our cellars, our weights, our
> measures, our promises, our protestations, our politic
> tricks and villanous Machiavelism, our enhancing
> of the prices of all commodities, and tell, whether
> the twelfth Psalm may not as fitly be applied to our
> times as to the days of the man of God; in which the

feigning, and lying, and facing, and guile, and subtlety of men provoked the psalmist to cry out, "Help, Lord; for there is not a godly man left: for the faithful are failed from among the children of men: they speak deceitfully every one with his neighbour, flattering with their lips, and speak with a double heart, which have said, With our tongue we will prevail; our lips are our own; who is Lord over us?"[4]

It may surprise you to know that he wrote that in 1612.

Will you join him, David, and us in a new kind of song? A song in which we as a people declare that the current way isn't okay, but that there is another way. And will we be the people who live that way? Look at your sphere of influence and ask God to help you live more justly, kindly, and graciously where you are, as an act of rebellion against the status quo.

Come on, church.

Prayer:

Father God, forgive us for being people who are often too comfortable in and with the world as it is. Remind us afresh of the call that you give us to be people of the Kingdom. We are meant to be the godly that the Psalmist was searching for. Equip us to be those types of people.

---

4. R. Wolcombe, quoted in Spurgeon, *The Treasury of David, Volume 1*, 145.

Psalm 13

Always Something to Sing About

Reading:

Take time to read the entire psalm, and then come back to read the following verses again.

> ⁵ *But I have trusted in your steadfast love;*
> *my heart shall rejoice in your salvation.*
> ⁶ *I will sing to the LORD,*
> *because he has dealt bountifully with me.*
> *Psalm 13:5–6*

Reflection:

David begins Psalm 13 in a very similar lamenting tone to the psalms that precede it. In fact, if you are someone who struggles with really dark moods, to the extent that it feels like God has abandoned you, then the first part of Psalm 13 might be like soothing nectar for your soul.

The psalm shifts dramatically toward the end, though, and that will be the focus of today's meditation. David found reason to sing, where before he could just sigh. He found reason to trust, where before he only doubted. He found reason to rejoice, where before he could only lament. What changed?

The truth is that none of his circumstances changed at all, but he paused and remembered the biggest truths of all. He remembered that God's love for him would never fail. He remembered that God was bringing him salvation and making him new. Lastly, he remembered that God was really good to him.

So here are some universal truths that apply to all who follow Christ, regardless of their circumstances.

God loves you in Christ, and His love for you will never fail.

> That you, being rooted and grounded in love, may have strength to comprehend with all the saints what is the breadth and length and height and depth, and to know the love of Christ that surpasses knowledge, that you may be filled with all the fullness of God.
>
> Ephesians 3:17b–19

God is the initiator and sustainer of your salvation through Jesus.

> Looking to Jesus, the founder and perfecter of our faith, who for the joy that was set before him endured the cross, despising the shame, and is seated at the right hand of the throne of God.
>
> Hebrew 12:2

God is really, really good to you already, and Jesus proves that.

> Blessed be the God and Father of our Lord Jesus Christ, who has blessed us in Christ with every spiritual blessing in the heavenly places.
>
> Ephesians 1:3

With all that in mind, rejoice, not in your circumstances, but in salvation.

Prayer:

Heavenly Father, forgive me for the times when I forget about your goodness toward me. Your kindness is undeserved and your mercy unearned. Give me eyes to see just how much blessing and grace you have poured out over me already through your Son. In Jesus's name, amen.

Psalm 14

Who's Fooling Who?

Reading:

Take time to read the entire psalm, and then come back to read the following verse.

> *The fool says in his heart, "There is no God."*
> *Psalm 14:1a*

Reflection:

There are some days in my life when I have moments of wondering if everything that I believe is true. They are usually fleeting moments, but they do happen.

Is this all really true? Am I giving my life to something that is just a myth? Is there really a God, and is He as good as the Scriptures say?

This is not something you will hear pastors or even Christians own up to all that often, but my suspicion is that most, if not all, people of faith have these moments. The key seems to be to have them less often, and for shorter periods of time. But how?

In Psalm 14, David suggests that a simple weighing of the evidence before you is enough to persuade you that faith isn't foolish. Lack of faith is.

This reminded me to just look back on my life at all the things God has done. When I simply examine what I have seen, and what I get to see every day, there is really only one conclusion I can come to.

There is a God, and He is good.

I have seen hopeless rebels come to a saving faith through a loving Savior. I have seen divorced couples, who could not be in the same room, find reconciling grace. I have seen victims of abuse find their power again with the strength that comes from forgiveness. I have seen wealthy men take off their suits to serve a family that has never known wealth. I have seen families mourn, but not as those who have no hope. And I have seen that rarest of things—people being changed, especially me.

The evidences of God's abundant grace are all around us. What do they look like in your life?

> For since the creation of the world God's invisible qualities—his eternal power and divine nature—have been clearly seen, being understood from what has been made, so that men are without excuse.
> Romans 1:20 (NIV)

Don't be a fool. Stop. Take a deep breath. Examine your life. Look up. He is there. He is good.

Prayer:

Heavenly Father, forgive me for the times when I doubt your goodness and for the times when I question your ongoing work in the world. Give me eyes to see who you are, and give me faith to trust in you more resolutely.

Psalm 15

How Good Is Good Enough?

Reading:

Take time to read the entire psalm.

> ^{1} O LORD, who shall sojourn in your tent?
>> Who shall dwell on your holy hill?
> ^{2} He who walks blamelessly and does what is right
>> and speaks truth in his heart;
> ^{3} who does not slander with his tongue
>> and does no evil to his neighbor,
>> nor takes up a reproach against his friend;
> ^{4} in whose eyes a vile person is despised,
>> but who honors those who fear the LORD;
>> who swears to his own hurt and does not change;
> ^{5} who does not put out his money at interest
>> and does not take a bribe against the innocent.
>> He who does these things shall never be moved.
>>> *Psalm 15:1-5*

Reflection:

Most theologians seem to agree that David wrote this psalm after he oversaw the work of moving the Ark of the Covenant to the holy hill of Zion. He had been confronted with the weight and glory of the holiness and magnificence of the very presence of God.

The Bible goes to great lengths to remind us that God isn't like us. He is good and gracious toward us, but His holiness and glory are fearful, worship-inducing elements that we would do well to remember. The sheer weight of the responsibility leaves David asking a question that many of us ask all the time.

How good is good enough for God? How good does one need to be in order to experience God's presence and favor?

David goes on to describe a man who lives a life that seems beyond what any of us could ever accomplish. Just be blameless and perfectly righteous and speak the truth all the time. Oh, okay, anything else? If that is the standard, then I am in trouble. David knows it, too, and the tone of this psalm is one of desperation.

The really good news is that God Himself provided that man. The man that David describes is Jesus, and He came to live the life that I could never live, on my behalf. Spurgeon, when talking about this psalm, says:

> On the grounds of law no mere man can dwell with God, for there is not one upon earth who answers to the just requirements mentioned in the succeeding verses. The questions in the text are asked of the Lord, as if none but the Infinite Mind could answer them so as to satisfy the unquiet conscience.[5]

The gospel isn't a declaration that I need to be good, but rather that Christ is already good, and has bestowed that goodness upon those who are no good. We then seek to live differently because of how good

---

5. Spurgeon, *The Treasury of David, Volume 1*, 34.

He has already shown us He is, rather than in the vain hope of us ourselves being good enough. We must obey to be sure, but as a result of His affection and not in an attempt to earn it. Spurgeon goes on:

> The Lord in answer to the question informs us by his Holy Spirit of the character of the man who alone can dwell in his holy hill. In perfection this holiness is found only in the Man of Sorrows, but in a measure it is wrought in all his people by the Holy Ghost.[6]

Being a Christian, therefore, is a declaration that you aren't good enough, but that Jesus is more than good enough on your behalf. That brings joy, freedom, and ironically a desire to be more Christ-like that is far more impactful than someone doing their best to live up to some imaginary benchmark.

> The gospel shows us a Law that must be fulfilled (destroying pride) and a Savior that fulfills it completely for us (destroying despair).[7]

Today, just remember: you're not okay. And that's okay, because He is more than okay.

Prayer:

Father God, your holiness is too otherworldly for me to ever comprehend. It is deeply humbling to consider that I will never live up to your perfect standards on my own. Thank you so much for sending your Son to live the life I never could so that I can be in right standing with you. Teach me to rely on Him and to trust Him and to pursue holiness. In His beautiful name I pray, amen.

---

6. Ibid., 177.

7. Timothy Keller, "Preaching Morality in an Amoral Age," in *The Art and Craft of Biblical Preaching: A Comprehensive Resource for Today's Commentators,* Haddon Robinson and Craig Brian Larson (Grand Rapids: Christianity Today International, 2005).

Psalm 16

Being Content with Your Lot

Reading:

Take time to read the entire psalm, and then come back to reflect on the following verses.

> ⁵ The LORD is my chosen portion and my cup;
>   you hold my lot.
> ⁶ The lines have fallen for me in pleasant places;
>   indeed, I have a beautiful inheritance.
>   Psalm 16:5–6

Reflection:

I grew up in a really happy, middle-income home. My parents were awesome in the way that they took care of us, and there was always abundant food on the table, both for us and for the continual flow of guests who joined us. I know now as an adult how hard they must have worked to make all that happen. As a kid, though, I really struggled to have a good perspective on how well my parents provided for my siblings and me. We weren't wealthy, and many of my friends were (or at least their parents were good at looking like they were).

I got laughed at by schoolmates for the fact that my sneakers had four stripes instead of the cool three, and most of my sports kit and school clothing were handed down to me from my brothers—one of whom was built like Papa Smurf, while the other was built like the beanstalk that Jack climbed.

I started resenting the kids who had more than I did. I felt hard done by, even though I had plenty. In hindsight, it was ridiculous, but it is how kids—and many adults—think (it is even more ridiculous to consider how my lifestyle compared to the vast majority of the population who grew up on the other side of apartheid). Yet, I still asked, "Why can't I be like the ones who have so much? How is it that some people are born into 'guaranteed' wealth and prosperity? What did they do to deserve their inheritance?"

Psalm 16 tells us that the children of God are people who have struck it rich every day of their lives. Regardless of how many stripes they have on their sneakers, they have an inheritance coming that is beyond description. The language that David uses in verses 5 and 6 describes a wealthy, good dad plotting out his kid's inheritance. He draws out the land on a piece of paper, and it looks abundant and generous. He then guarantees it as a secure possession that no one can take from his child.

That's what God has done for us.

That's what's coming for the children of God.

There is a magnificent inheritance from the Father that no one can take, waste, spend, or steal. What have we done to deserve that inheritance? Nothing. Paris Hilton has worked hard for what she has coming to her, compared to what we have done for what we get in Christ. The real trick is to weigh your life in light of that guaranteed inheritance, instead of killing yourself trying to establish one here that can be taken away in a moment.

God your Father loves you. Enough to make you part of the family and include you in the inheritance. Trust Him. Be content with your lot. That, according to the Scriptures, is a great gain (1 Tim. 6:6).

Prayer:

Father God, forgive me for the times I only see what I don't have and fail to see the inheritance you have granted me. Teach me to live in such a way in this life that shows I trust you for the next life. In Jesus's name we pray, amen.

Psalm 17

God's Pupil

Reading:

Take time to read the entire psalm, and then come back to read the
following verse again.

> *Keep me as the apple of your eye;*
> *hide me in the shadow of your wings.*
> *Psalm 17:8*

Reflection:

Psalm 17 returns us to more lamenting from David. I find this strangely
encouraging, as we are often quite hard on ourselves in terms of our
ability to grow in grace and spiritual maturity. I, for one, would love
to see progress at a more rapid rate than I currently experience. The
Psalms show us that while David was a man after God's own heart, his
circumstances were tough for long periods of his life, and his spiritual
journey was often a dark and seemingly slow one.

There is one verse in Psalm 17 that brings incredible hope, though.
David pleads with God to keep him as the apple of His eye (v. 8). That
means he was already the apple of God's eye. He was only praying that
he would remain so. That is amazing.

The apple was the ancients' way of referring to the pupil. It was seen as the most precious part of the body that was to be protected above all else. David suggests that God protects His children, like the body protects the pupil. High cheekbones shelter it from incoming blows. Bushy eyebrows keep sweat from getting in. Eyelashes act like fences, keeping all unwanted intruders out, and eyelids can shut to provide rest and quiet.

God treats His children like that. He is like a mother bird, standing with His mighty wings outstretched, sheltering us chicks from harm (v. 8b). He has already proved this to us by allowing His Son to stretch His arms out on the cross to protect us from the harm of our sin and rebellion.

Are you struggling to know how God sees you today? Maybe, just maybe, like David, you are the apple of His eye. He has got you covered.

Prayer:

Father God, keep me as the apple of your eye. Thank you for the way you protect us and care for us. Give me eyes to see the many ways you are always doing this for us, and the ultimate way you already have done it through your Son.

In Jesus's name, amen.

Psalm 18

Tough Day at the Office?

Reading:

Take time to read the entire psalm (it is long, but well worth it), and then come back to read the following verses again.

> *¹ I love you, O LORD, my strength.*
> *² The LORD is my rock and my fortress and my deliverer,*
>   *my God, my rock, in whom I take refuge,*
>   *my shield, and the horn of my salvation, my stronghold.*
> *³ I call upon the LORD, who is worthy to be praised,*
>   *and I am saved from my enemies.*
>   *Psalm 18:1–3*

Reflection:

I have one of the best jobs in the world, working with some of the best people in the world to proclaim the best news in the world, but even with all that in mind, I am not immune to tough days in the office. Even when I have witnessed the incredible things we get to see every single Sunday in services, Mondays in the office can seem overwhelming.

David wrote Psalm 18 right at the zenith of his kingly leadership. He was leading one of the most powerful nations in the region, a nation that had the additional burden of being the people of God, and David knew that war was approaching from without and mutiny was approaching from within. If I am tempted to think my job is stressful, I have to remember that my son hasn't tried to kill me recently (as David's son was attempting to do), and I don't have to lead the most pigheaded and rebellious people on the planet.

So, what did David go to in order to provide him with comfort, faith, and even joy on his most difficult and troublesome days as king?

He looked back to the unchanging nature of God and allowed his view of the world to be shaped by who God is rather than by what he would be facing. It's a helpful thing to do.

He declared that God was his strength, and he knew that God never gets tired of being strong. This means that David was free to be weak.

He declared that God was his rock, so he knew that he stood on solid ground.

He declared that God was his fortress, so he knew that he was safe and secure in his presence.

He declared that God was his deliverer, so he knew that he would be rescued from his enemies, and he would be saved from himself.

He declared that God was a shield, so he knew that the blows of the enemy and his fiery darts of accusation couldn't pierce him.

He declared that God's salvation was like a horn with which he could take ground. He didn't just need to defend. He could use the gospel to assault the dark places.

He declared that God was worthy of praise.

He just declared.

So, what will you look to in order to shape your worldview? Will you look to your surrounding circumstances, or will you look to your unchanging God and declare that He is, in fact, all the things that

David said He was, and still is? The choice you make will determine how you get through your toughest days.

Prayer:

Father God, forgive me for the days when I let circumstances determine my faith in your goodness rather than letting my faith in your goodness determine my approach to my circumstances. Gift me greater faith, please, Lord.

Psalm 19

Starry Starry Night

Reading:

Take time to read the entire psalm, and then come back to read the following verses again.

> ¹ *The heavens declare the glory of God,*
> *and the sky above proclaims his handiwork.*
> ² *Day to day pours out speech,*
> *and night to night reveals knowledge.*
> ³ *There is no speech, nor are there words,*
> *whose voice is not heard.*
> ⁴ *Their voice goes out through all the earth,*
> *and their words to the end of the world.*
> *Psalm 19:1–4*

Reflection:

I love living in the city. I was born and raised in the big, sometimes bad, city of Johannesburg, and I love the pace, the pulse, and the tension you get in what people call "the big smoke." Having said all that, I love getting out of the city every now and then as well. One of the reasons for this is that it allows me to get out of the smog and smoke so that I can have an uninhibited view of the stars at night. There are few things better than sitting next to an African bushveld fire and looking up at a clear sky. It is always a humbling and worshipful experience. It makes me and my circumstances feel very small, and that is a good thing.

David tells us in Psalm 19 that it is by God's design that the night sky should lead to worship. The stars yell out at us that God is good and in control. Paul tells us in Romans 1 that clues like this to God's magnificence leave every man without excuse. All you need to do to know that there is a God, and that He is good, is to look up every now and then.

The size and scope of the universe is staggering, yet when Moses documents how it was made, he says:

> He made the stars also.
> Genesis 1:16 (KJV).

Nothing is too difficult for our God. Look up.

Prayer:

Our Father in heaven, you have displayed your goodness and your power in the skies for all of us to see. Forgive us for forgetting to look up now and then. We pray, with your servant David, that our response to your majesty would be a humble and obedient one.

> Let the words of my mouth and the meditation of my
> heart be acceptable in your sight,
> O Lord, my rock and my redeemer.
> Psalm 19:14

Psalm 20

Sing Like You're Winning

Reading:

Take time to read the entire psalm, and then come back to read the following verses.

> [5] *May we shout for joy over your salvation,*
> *and in the name of our God set up our banners!*
> *May the LORD fulfill all your petitions!*
> [6] *Now I know that the LORD saves his anointed;*
> *he will answer him from his holy heaven*
> *with the saving might of his right hand.*
> [7] *Some trust in chariots and some in horses,*
> *but we trust in the name of the LORD our God.*
> *Psalm 20:5–7*

Reflection:

I enjoy watching English Premier League football. It is full of contradictions and irony. The totally overpaid super athlete, who falls over easier than a tired toddler, and who displays a similar level of maturity when he fails to get his way. The foul-mouth ranting of a so-called captain, who happens to be wearing an armband that has the word "respect" emblazoned on it. It's all rather hilarious. But the biggest contradiction by far is the fierce, out-of-shape fans, who look like they ate a football, shouting and screaming and hurling insults at said super athlete for his apparent inability to do something with a football that they could never accomplish in their lives. I love these fans. They are passionate, and committed, and sold out to their cause. They seem to genuinely believe that their involvement in the game makes a difference, and it probably does. What this means is that you can actually tell who is winning a football game by the volume of the songs and the section of the stands from which the song comes. Fans sing loud from both sides when it is 0–0. But when one side scores, their fans go through the roof and sing taunts toward the other fans about what losers they are. Again, there is some irony here, but it's fun to watch.

Psalm 20 is literally a war cry, a song that would be sung by the community before Israel went to war. It was sung in the hope of victory, and it was sung full of faith. It was also sung in the knowledge that one day they would have a King who would liberate His people forever.

That King arrived. His name was Jesus.

So, this got me thinking. We know that King Jesus has already come. We know that the ultimate battle has already been won. The game isn't even close.

IT IS FINISHED!

In light of that, shouldn't we be people who shout for joy and raise up banners in victory? If the world were watching us as a set of cheering fans, I think they may assume we are losing, or on our best day it could look like a draw. That's a sad indictment.

The apostle Paul said that what Christ did on the cross was nothing short of a landslide victory against His enemies, and that when He rose from the dead, He led an open-top bus tour through the streets, parading the fact that He had won, and that everyone on His team had therefore also won (Col. 2:15).

This song is written with the group of believers in mind. It is written for the collective. So, next time you are together as a group, on a Sunday, why not make a commitment to sing like we're winning? Because we are. Because He has.

Prayer:

Father God, teach me to be someone who raises banners and lifts up shouts of joy because of your great salvation. Forgive me for getting more excited over things that don't matter than I get about the things that really matter.

Psalm 21

I'm Not Shaking

Reading:

Take time to read the entire psalm, and then come back to read the following verses.

> 6 *For you make him most blessed forever;*
>   *you make him glad with the joy of your presence.*
> 7 *For the king trusts in the LORD,*
>   *and through the steadfast love of the Most High*
>   *he shall not be moved.*
>
>   *Psalm 21:6–7*

Reflection:

Psalm 21 is the second half of a coupled pair. It follows on from Psalm 20 and continues to thank God for the awesome victory He brings. Verses 6 and 7 are striking and worth another look.

David is speaking about the different ways God has blessed him and brought him victory as a covenant son of God, so the things he mentions in these verses can be said to extend in a way to all of God's covenant children.

He has granted us eternal blessings (v. 6a), which include an eternity with Him, a guaranteed inheritance in heaven, a place in the family of God, a seat at the table of the wedding supper of the Lamb, and eternal, unhindered access to the astonishing presence of the Most High God. We stress so much in this life because we don't think nearly enough about what is waiting for us in the next.

God doesn't just leave us with only future hope of blessing, though. He also gives us the joy of His presence in this life (v. 6b). This is astonishing, and something I don't think I appreciate all that much.

> God.
> With me.
> Around me.
> In me.
> All the time.

I can't help but think of how much more joy I would have if I remembered that more often than I do.

Last, David speaks of God's unfailing love (v. 7). This is still something I am getting my head and heart around. When I read the Scriptures, I am absolutely persuaded that God loves other people and that His love for them is unfailing and unlimited. But where I struggle is in believing He feels that way about me.

> He loves me.
> That doesn't change.
> That doesn't fail.

Because His love for me is based on His goodness and not mine, He doesn't withdraw it from me when I fail.

So just like King David, I trust in the Lord. He is good to me. I shall not be moved.

Prayer:

Father God, you have blessed me far more than I deserve through the gift of your salvation and the power of your presence. Give me eyes to see just how steadfast your love is toward me, and give me the faith to trust in it regardless of what I am going through.

Psalm 22

The Magnificent Weight of Calvary

Reading:

Take the time to read this entire psalm slowly and thoughtfully, and then come back to read the following verse.

> *My God, my God, why have you forsaken me?*
> *Why are you so far from saving me, from the words of my groaning?*
>
> *Psalm 22:1*

Reflection:

I love the Bible. I enjoy reading it, but truth be told, I feel like most of the time it reads me. It is a living and active work, indeed. Sometimes, though, you come across a passage that is so weighty, so intense, so heart-wrenching, that you literally want to slam the book shut before the words trample over you. Psalm 22 is one of those passages.

Before the Scriptures had chapter numbering, the Psalms were known and referred to by their first line and not by their number. When Jesus cried out "My God, my God, why have you forsaken me?"

from the cross, as recorded in Matthew 27:46, all of the Jews in earshot would have known He was drawing their attention to Psalm 22. He was crying out to those who were listening, that Psalm 22 was about Him. Many would have been horrified as they realized that Jesus was the prophesied suffering servant so vividly described in that psalm.

Do yourself a favor and read the entire psalm; then read Matthew 27. It is incredible how the crucifixion fulfills everything that was promised. One was spoken about who would bring new hope to all nations, and He did it by being brutally assassinated on a Roman tree. He bought our redemption by being our sacrifice.

Just look at what He did.

> He was forsaken (v. 1) so that we can experience everlasting faithfulness.
> He was ignored (v. 2) so that our prayers will always be answered.
> He was scorned and despised (v. 6) so that we can experience deep love.
> He was mocked (v. 7) so that we can be unashamed.
> He was poured out (v. 14) so that we can be filled up by His Spirit.
> He experienced dislocation (v. 14) so that we can be grafted into a new body.
> He had a broken heart (v. 14) so that we can walk in wholeness.
> He was weak (v. 15) so that our strength can rise.
> He was surrounded by evil (v. 16) so that we can experience His surrounding protection.

> Oh, the weight.
> Our crucified King.
> Look at what He has done.

Prayer:

Oh, Father, when I pause to think that your Son was forsaken so that I could be brought into your family, I am overwhelmed. Teach me, Lord, to dwell in the shadow of your Son's wonderful cross.

Psalm 23

Dumb, Dumb Sheep

Reading:

Read the entire psalm. It is very familiar to many of us, so take the time to read it slowly and thoughtfully.

> [1] *The LORD is my shepherd; I shall not want.*
> [2] *He makes me lie down in green pastures.*
>   *He leads me beside still waters.*
> [3] *He restores my soul.*
>   *He leads me in paths of righteousness*
>   *for his name's sake.*
> [4] *Even though I walk through the valley of the shadow of death,*
>   *I will fear no evil,*
>   *for you are with me;*
>   *your rod and your staff,*
>   *they comfort me.*
> [5] *You prepare a table before me*
>   *in the presence of my enemies;*
>   *you anoint my head with oil;*
>   *my cup overflows.*

> [6] *Surely goodness and mercy shall follow me*
>   *all the days of my life,*
>   *and I shall dwell in the house of the* LORD
>   *forever.*
>
>   *Psalm 23:1-6*

Reflection:

The Bible talks about sheep a lot, and they are often the animal of choice when metaphorically describing mankind.

> All we all like sheep have gone astray.
>   Isaiah 53:6

> When he saw the crowds, he had compassion for them, because they were harassed and helpless, like sheep without a shepherd.
>   Matthew 9:36

Psalm 23 again intimates that we are like sheep, but that we have a good shepherd in God. I used to think this was very endearing. I could understand why we print this psalm on coffee cups and bookmarks to encourage us. We are like fluffy little lambs, and that seems like a very sweet way to refer to people.

A few years ago, though, Sue and I had the wonderful opportunity to stay on a working sheep farm in Wales for a couple of days. My understanding of sheep changed completely. They are the dumbest and most helpless of all animals. They can literally do nothing for themselves. If they aren't herded to new pastures by a dog and a shepherd, they won't go. If they aren't sheared by a shearer, their wool will grow larger and heavier until they fall over and can't get up, and they get pecked to death by ravens. They are utterly helpless. Tasty, to be sure, but helpless.

Psalm 23 suggests we are the same. We cannot help ourselves, and our efforts to do so often end up with more destructive results. Fortunately, we have a loving and caring shepherd who looks after us.

He makes me lie down, because I don't know how to rest. He leads me to living water, because I don't know how to find real sustenance. He guides me on the right path, because without Him I would get hopelessly lost. He protects me from danger, because I am oblivious to the threat.

I am nothing but a dumb sheep, but He is a truly wonderful Shepherd. He does it all, not just for me, but "for His name's sake" (v. 3), and I am totally fine with that. Thank God that He doesn't leave me to my own devices. I would fall over and be raven food.

Prayer:

Father God, I acknowledge that I am totally dependent on you for everything I need. Forgive me for the way I stray and the ways in which I try to live without your leading me. Teach me to lie down and to enjoy the green pastures you provide for me. Amen.

Psalm 24

Open the Door

Reading:

Take time to read the entire psalm, and then come back to read the following verses.

> [7] *Lift up your heads, O gates!*
> *And be lifted up, O ancient doors,*
> *That the King of glory may come in.*
> [8] *Who is this King of glory?*
> *The LORD, strong and mighty,*
> *the LORD, mighty in battle!*
> [9] *Lift up your heads, O gates!*
> *And lift them up, O ancient doors,*
> *that the King of glory may come in.*
> [10] *Who is this King of glory?*
> *The LORD of hosts,*
> *he is the King of glory! Selah*
> *Psalm 24:7–10*

Reflection:

The ancient cities were surrounded by massive walls and enormous gates designed to keep them safe from attack. In this psalm, most believe that David was bringing the Ark of the Covenant, which contained the very presence of God Himself, into the city of Jerusalem to dwell with His people (2 Sam. 6). In order for Him to get in, though, they needed to temporarily render the city vulnerable by opening the gates, so that the King of Glory could come in. The song was written as a call and response supposed to be sung in two parts. The one part would be the guards at the gate, shouting out, "Who is the King? Are you sure you have the right credentials for us to open up these gates?" The response would be from David, who was leading a praise party, shouting back, "This is the Lord Almighty we are talking about."

When Jesus speaks to the church at Laodicea in Revelation 3:20, He says, "Here I am! I stand at the door and knock. If anyone hears my voice and opens the door, I will come in and eat with him, and he with me" (NIV). I have often heard this passage taught as an invitation to salvation, but Jesus is clearly speaking to people who are already part of the church. They are followers of Christ, albeit not particularly good ones. He tells them, and I believe He tells us, that He desires greater intimacy with His people. He wants to dwell with us, and eat with us, and commune with us. He is knocking, but we have to open.

I am a lot like the guards in Psalm 24. I am scared to open up, to lift up the gates, to render myself vulnerable even for a moment. David is reminding me that the one knocking is good, and glorious, and altogether trustworthy, and if I open the gates, He will come in, and I won't regret it for a second.

What are the gates that keep you safe, but keep you from a greater experience of the presence of God? Lift them up! Let the King of Glory in!

Prayer:

Father God, forgive me for the ways that I don't open myself up to you in vulnerability, and don't acknowledge my constant need for you and your powerful presence. Teach me what it means to open up and to let you, the King of Glory, manifest in power and glory in my life. In Jesus's mighty name, amen.

Psalm 25

Storytellers

Reading:

Take time to read the entire psalm, and then come back to read the following verses.

> [6] *Remember your mercy, O LORD, and your steadfast love,*
> *for they have been from of old.*
> [7] *Remember not the sins of my youth or my transgressions;*
> *according to your steadfast love remember me,*
> *for the sake of your goodness, O LORD!*
> *Psalm 25:6–7*

Reflection:

Not that long ago, I met with a bunch of my good guy friends to celebrate the birth of two baby boys in our community. We feasted, we laughed, we dreamed of futures, and we remembered our pasts. When men get together without the stabilizing sanity and desire for accurate detail in storytelling a lot of women seem to have, the stories of the past can become quite elaborate. All of the feats accomplished are amplified in the retelling, and most of the sins committed are minimized or brushed aside as part of our rite of passage. But this time, as tale after tale of my epic, extended adolescent rebellion was told, I found myself becoming distinctly uncomfortable. "Did I really do that? Why? Did I really have the reputation as that kind of guy?" Even though it was a really good night out, I left feeling condemned and ashamed of the way I had acted as a youth. Behind the laughs was a deep hurt. I should have known better. I shouldn't have done those things. I should have been leading my group of friends toward Christ instead of away from Him.

This psalm then came at just the right time. David was a bit older when he wrote it and was looking back at his life, pleading with God to not remember him according to his rebellion. David didn't want the things he had done to define him. He wanted to be remembered by another standard, and not the standard that he had set, because he'd done some shameful things.

He wanted God to forget his sins. He wanted God to measure him against God's own goodness, mercy, and love, instead of against his own rebellion.

Guess what? God answered his prayer. David talks about it in Psalm 103.

> ⁸ The LORD is merciful and gracious,
>   slow to anger and abounding in steadfast love.
> ⁹ He will not always chide,
>   nor will he keep his anger forever.
> ¹⁰ He does not deal with us according to our sins,
>   nor repay us according to our iniquities.
> ¹¹ For as high as the heavens are above the earth,
>   so great is his steadfast love toward those who fear him;
> ¹² as far as the east is from the west,
>   so far does he remove our transgressions from us.
> ¹³ As a father shows compassion to his children,
>   so the LORD shows compassion to those who fear him.
>   Psalm 103:8–13

What I did doesn't define me. What may have been done to me doesn't define me either. I am defined by the longstanding, constant, and unshakable love of God, who chooses to remember me based on His faithfulness and not my rebellion. Because of that, David declares.

> Indeed, none who wait for you
> shall be put to shame.
> Psalm 25:3

Now, that's a story worth telling.

Prayer:

Father God, I am ashamed of many things I have done. I pray that you remember them no more and that you instead remember your mercy. Thank you for your grace. Teach me to live with confidence and certainty in your forgiveness. Jesus secured that, and so it is in His name I pray, amen.

Psalm 26

Meaningless Meetings?

Reading:

Take time to read the entire psalm, and then come back to read the following verses again.

> ⁶ *I wash my hands in innocence*
>   *and go around your altar, O LORD,*
> ⁷ *proclaiming thanksgiving aloud,*
>   *and telling all your wondrous deeds.*
>   *Psalm 26:6–7*

Reflection:

The church is a living organism of people, not a building or a gathering or service. We know and affirm that continually. However, there is something special that happens when the church gathers together in one place. The people of God have always been encouraged to have regular gatherings. It's like God wants to remind us we are better together than we are apart.

But liturgies (every church has them) and celebrity pastor culture have meant that these gatherings have often amounted to nothing more than 99 percent of the people present either shouting for or shouting at the 1 percent who "do church" for them. This is obviously not the way it was supposed to be.

In Psalm 26, David gives us great input about some of the things that make a gathering of believers special and dynamic. My recommendation is that we all try to do these things when we gather, and I believe we will start to experience much more meaningful gatherings week in and week out, and I also believe that the gates of hell tremble at the thought of that.

So here they are, five things from Psalm 26 that we should do at every church gathering:

1.   Prepare ourselves for what God wants to say to us (v. 2).

In our crazy, busy lives, we leave very little space for contemplation and introspection. We carry this over into church gatherings, where we rush in at the last possible moment, endure the jam-packed program, and then rush out again, leaving little time for the Spirit of God to whisper to us and change us. How about arriving a little early and spending some time in prayer asking God to speak to you and change you? That way, you won't spend the first two songs catching your breath and grumbling at your spouse for making you late.

2.   Get some truth (v. 3).

We believe that the Bible is true and that it is living, active, and useful for today. As preachers, we don't claim to have a monopoly on truth in our church, but we are committed to doing our best to get to the meaning of the text, and to convey that faithfully. What will help you a lot as a discerning hearer will be to engage the text yourself. Read in anticipation, and ask the Spirit of God to reveal truth to you. Actively engage the sermon and the text that it is preached from.

3.   Repent of sin and receive grace (v. 6).

I love the image that David uses of washing his hands as a declaration of innocence. He does this at the altar, where sacrifices for sin were made. This isn't David trying to pretend he hasn't sinned. This is the joy that comes from owning up to sin and finding God's grace, thanks to the sacrifice Christ made for us once and for all.

Repentance leads to joy—don't try to hide your sin from God, and don't believe that acknowledging it will make you feel guilty. The opposite is true. Martin Luther said, "When our Lord and Master Jesus Christ said 'Repent,' He called for the entire life of believers to be one of repentance."[8] We should repent every time we gather. It's a beautiful act of faith and a declaration of dependence.

4. Sing as loud as you can (v. 7a).

There are only a couple of occasions in the Psalms when David will talk about singing beautifully or skillfully. There are lots of references to singing loudly, though. It is absolutely pointless to stand passive and let the band sing. It literally makes no sense. If this story about God is true, He is worthy of praise. We shouldn't withhold it. We should sing as loud as we can.

5. Testify to God's goodness (v. 7b).

One of the glorious things about being part of a people is that we get to spur each other on. One of the ways to do this is to tell each other of God's faithfulness.

If we did all these things at our gatherings, I am persuaded that the surrounding community would be impacted, because we would start to become the city on the hill that cannot be hidden, and we would all scatter after we have gathered with the light of the gospel as our guide.

Prayer:

Father God, teach us the significance of gathering with others in your name. Change us, Lord, into a people who glorify you in our gatherings. In Jesus's name, amen.

8. Martin Luther, The 95 Theses.

Psalm 27

Fear Factor

Reading:

Take time to read the entire psalm, and then come back to read the following verses again.

> [1] *The LORD is my light and my salvation;*
>   *whom shall I fear?*
> *The LORD is the stronghold of my life;*
>   *of whom shall I be afraid?*
> [2] *When evildoers assail me*
>   *to eat up my flesh,*
>   *my adversaries and foes,*
>   *it is they who stumble and fall.*
> [3] *Though an army encamp against me,*
>   *my heart shall not fear;*
>   *though war arise against me,*
>   *yet I will be confident.*
>   *Psalm 27:1–3*

Reflection:

In Psalm 27 David asks some questions based on logic that are really helpful for us. If God is who He says He is, what do we possibly have to be afraid of? If He brings salvation, what condemnation should I fear? If He is the stronghold of my life, what earthly threat is so scary? I couldn't help but think of Romans 8:31-39 when I read this.

> What, then, shall we say in response to this? If God is for us, who can be against us? He who did not spare his own Son, but gave him up for us all—how will he not also, along with him, graciously give us all things? Who will bring any charge against those whom God has chosen? It is God who justifies. Who is he that condemns? Christ Jesus, who died—more than that, who was raised to life—is at the right hand of God and is also interceding for us. Who shall separate us from the love of Christ? Shall trouble or hardship or persecution or famine or nakedness or danger or sword? As it is written:
>> "For your sake we face death all day long; we are considered as sheep to be slaughtered."
>
> No, in all these things we are more than conquerors through him who loved us. For I am convinced that neither death nor life, neither angels nor demons, neither the present nor the future, nor any powers, neither height nor depth, nor anything else in all creation, will be able to separate us from the love of God that is in Christ Jesus our Lord.

Read the whole passage again. Slowly. Deliberately.

If the Scripture is true, and if you are a child of God, then God is for you, and you have nothing to be afraid of. He is so for you that He gave up His own Son. He doesn't need to prove it again through your circumstances, He has proved it once and for all. I know that seems like an overly simplistic view of the world and is in no way an attempt to minimize or nullify what you are going through, but it is an encouragement to look to the One bigger than whatever you are going through.

He is for you, and that is why the most common command in Scripture is,

DO NOT BE AFRAID!

Prayer:

Father God, forgive me for the times I have failed to trust in your unfailing love toward me. Teach me to fear you and nothing else. Keep my eyes fixed on you, and keep me always trusting in your salvation. Amen.

Psalm 28

A Pastor's Prayer

Reading:

Take time to read the entire psalm, and then come back to read the following verses again.

> 6 *Blessed be the LORD!*
> *For he has heard the voice of my pleas for mercy.*
> 7 *The LORD is my strength and my shield;*
> *in him my heart trusts, and I am helped;*
> *my heart exults, and with my song I give thanks to him.*
> 8 *The LORD is the strength of his people;*
> *he is the saving refuge of his anointed.*
> 9 *Oh, save your people and bless your heritage!*
> *Be their shepherd and carry them forever.*
> *Psalm 28:6–9*

Reflection:

Psalm 28 is a pretty personal one to me. I identify with so much of David's personal spiritual struggle in prayer. I love how up and down he can be. I also love how he shifts from praying for himself to praying for the people that God has asked him to lead.

As a pastor, I pray for the people under my care all the time, and a lot of the things that I ask for are found in the final parts of Psalm 28.

So here is how Psalm 28 goes in my words. Please note that I am not trying to improve on Scripture, and I am not claiming to be inspired. The Scripture is perfect and objective, but it is also deeply personal, and so this is what this psalm feels like to me. I find it quite helpful to pray the Psalms, so this is Psalm 28 as a personal prayer for me. Maybe try re-writing it as a prayer for you.

Prayer:

Dear Lord,

I am really tired of my prayers bouncing off the ceiling.

Please answer me, because if you don't I am going to be a wreck.

I really need your mercy, and I am desperate to feel your forgiveness because my sin weighs so heavily on me.

Please expose the wicked deeds of those who seek to bring violence, division, and hatred into our land and our community. Expose our own hearts when we are the perpetrators of this sort of wickedness against others.

I love you, and I am so thankful for what you have done for me. As I look back at my life, I realize you have always been listening, always been forgiving, always been protecting, and always been guiding. Even when it felt like you weren't there, you were. As a result, I want to worship you freely and boldly. It seems lame and ungrateful to keep my hands in my pockets, when I should throw them up in praise when I think of all you have done.

Now please, God, look after your people in the church. Let their children worship you and their children's children, too. I can't take care of them, Lord, but you can look after them. They are yours. They listen to you. Please protect them from harm.

In Jesus's name, amen.

Psalm 29

The Theology of Thunder

Reading:

Take time to read the entire psalm, and then come back to read the following verses again.

> ³ *The voice of the LORD is over the waters;*
>   *the God of glory thunders,*
>   *the LORD, over many waters.*
> ⁴ *The voice of the LORD is powerful;*
>   *the voice of the LORD is full of majesty.*
> ⁵ *The voice of the LORD breaks the cedars;*
>   *the LORD breaks the cedars of Lebanon.*
> ⁶ *He makes Lebanon to skip like a calf,*
>   *and Sirion like a young wild ox.*
> ⁷ *The voice of the LORD flashes forth flames of fire.*
> ⁸ *The voice of the LORD shakes the wilderness;*
>   *the LORD shakes the wilderness of Kadesh.*
> ⁹ *The voice of the LORD makes the deer give birth*
>   *and strips the forests bare,*
>   *and in his temple all cry, "Glory!"*
>   *Psalm 29:3–9*

Reflection:

I am very fortunate to live in such an incredible city. Johannesburg is truly a remarkable place. She has major issues, to be sure, but we love calling her home in this season of our lives.

One of the best things about the city is the weather. It is sunny most days, and when it rains, it tends to rain with purpose, and the purpose seems to be the destruction of all things. Then it stops, and it is sunny again. The thunderstorms in Johannesburg are epic. It's not the hippy, cuddly kind of rain you get in Seattle, or London, or Cape Town. You can watch the storms coming for a long time. You can smell them getting closer. You can literally feel the electric charge in the air, and then you get that distinctive sound. Thunder. Coming closer.

It is impossible to feel significant whilst in the midst of a thunderstorm. Whatever your worldview is, you simply cannot place yourself at the center of it all when it seems like the sky is trying to destroy the earth. You just have to feel small.

In Psalm 29, David says that he knows what that feels like. The thunder is like the voice of the Lord, and everything compared to it feels small and powerless. It is by design, because I think we often forget who we are dealing with when we deal with God. He is loving, and faithful, and kind, and merciful. That is absolutely true. But He is also sovereign, and eternal, and righteous, and magnificent, and majestic, and glorious, and absolutely worthy of praise, adoration, worship, and wonder.

This is why David says that our only response is to:

> ¹ Ascribe to the Lord, O heavenly beings,
>   ascribe to the Lord glory and strength.
> ² Ascribe to the Lord the glory due his name;
>   worship the Lord in the splendor of holiness.
> Psalm 29:1–2

It is a good thing to remember and declare how huge God is. It gives us the space to be small and to be okay with that. A small God would be bad news for everybody.

Next time you hear thunder. Ascribe. He made it all. He is worthy of worship.

Prayer:

Father God, forgive me for the times that I have acted as if you are small, when in reality your voice thunders over the waters. Teach me to trust in your power, majesty, and might. In Jesus's name, amen.

Psalm 30

Momentary Anger, Lifelong Favor

Reading:

Take time to read the entire psalm, and then come back to read the following verses again.

> ⁴ *Sing praises to the* LORD, *O you his saints,*
>   *and give thanks to his holy name*
> ⁵ *For his anger is but for a moment,*
>   *and his favor is for a lifetime.*
> *Weeping may tarry for the night,*
>   *But joy comes with the morning.*
>   *Psalm 30:4–5*

Reflection:

If I were God, I would have given up on me long ago. My propensity for repeat folly and rebellion is nothing short of astonishing, and it often leaves me feeling as if I may have reached the bottom of the well of God's grace.

"He can't forgive me for that again, surely? Can He?"

The Scripture is clear from the beginning until the end that God is vehemently opposed to sin. In fact, it says time and time again that

He is wrathfully opposed to it, and even offended and grieved by it. It makes Him angry when we continuously rebel. I can't deny that from Scripture. The cross stands as ultimate proof of His opposition to sin.

But it also says some amazing stuff about His anger and wrath. It says that He is slow to anger. In other words, He has a long wick, even though we test it continually. Psalm 30 tells us the great news that His anger only lasts a moment. A moment! I get the sulks for days when people sin against me.

God doesn't hold onto His anger toward my rebellion. That's amazing.

But it is even better than that. He pours out favor and grace again and again and again and again (v. 5a). He doesn't just forgive my sin repeatedly—He actually pours out blessing on me repeatedly. The weight of my sin brings some weeping in the night, to be sure, but the certainty of God's new mercies and everlasting favor leads to lots of rejoicing in the morning (v. 5b).

If this is true, then we should be people who are quick to repent and quick to forgive others. The grace and favor of God must change us.

Quit your sulking if you have sinned. You failed. God forgave, and there is favor waiting to be received. Believe that, and rejoice.

Prayer:

Father God, thank you for your anger against sin. That anger was poured out for a moment on your Son so that I could enjoy the favor that lasts a lifetime. Teach me to repent quickly and fully when I sin, trusting in your total forgiveness and living with joy as an act of faith in your forgiving work.

Psalm 31

God Has a Massive Reputation at Stake

Reading:

Take time to read the entire psalm, and then come back to read the following verses again.

> *² Incline your ear to me;*
> *rescue me speedily!*
> *Be a rock of refuge for me,*
> *a strong fortress to save me!*
> *³ For you are my rock and my fortress;*
> *and for your name's sake you lead me and guide me;*
> *⁴ you take me out of the net they have hidden for me,*
> *for you are my refuge.*
> *⁵ Into your hand I commit my spirit;*
> *you have redeemed me, O LORD, faithful God.*
>
> *Psalm 31:2–5*

Reflection:

I know I have said this before in these meditations, but I really love David. Time and time again, in the Psalms he explains that God will not abandon him. Time and time again, he speaks clearly of God's goodness and faithfulness. Yet, time and time again, he cries out to God to be faithful, and time and time again he cries out, pleading that God will never abandon him. I love that kind of certain uncertainty.

I experience a lot of that certain uncertainty myself. I know, but I don't always feel like I know.

Quite a few times in the Psalms, in the midst of this pleading, David appeals to God to deliver him based on something we don't often hear about in churches and pulpits today. David asks God to protect God's own name (Ps. 33:3b, 23:3b). David asks God to remember that God's own reputation is on the line in David's reputation.

David asks God to be about God.

This is strangely comforting, but it takes a while to sink in. We have been lured into thinking that God is about us. Now, let's be clear: He is for us and He undoubtedly loves us. But He is not about us, and, trust me, that is really good news.

How?

If God is about me, the pressure is all on me. I need to be a success in order for God to be deemed good and desirable. If I am not a success, I just need to pretend to be one. Sounds a lot like church, doesn't it? And how long will God be patient with me while I am not a success? What is my timeframe for pulling myself up by my bootstraps, and doing well like all these other people seem to be doing? If it is about me, then it is all very insecure and uncertain.

If God is about God, then it is all on Him. Then He will never abandon me, because His name is riding on it. Then I don't have to succeed, and I can be honest about it, because it enhances His reputation when a guy like me continually fails, and continually gets grace, and continually sees God working through my ineptitude, in spite of myself. That is really comforting.

God is about God. My part in the story is tiny. The pressure is off me.

Prayer:

So, Heavenly Father, please, for the sake of your great name, don't ever abandon me. Please continue to put up with me for as long as it brings you glory to do so. And please, help me play my tiny part well, so that your reputation will be enhanced. In Jesus's glorious name I pray, amen.

Psalm 32

The Stuck Record of the Gospel Sounds Beautiful

Introduction and Reading:

I preach the gospel for a living, so you would think I would have gotten used to it by now, but when I read passages like Psalm 32 I am totally overwhelmed afresh by the good news. I know I will sound like a stuck record, going on about the goodness and sweetness of God's mercy toward us, but honestly, I never get tired of listening to that record, and I don't think you should, either.

Read the whole of Psalm 32, slowly, and then come back to read the following verses again.

> *¹ Blessed is the one whose transgression is forgiven,*
> *   whose sin is covered.*
> *² Blessed is the man against whom the* LORD *counts no iniquity,*
> *   and in whose spirit there is no deceit.*
> *   Psalm 32:1–2*

Reflection:

The historians and theologians reckon that David wrote this shortly after his repentance that he outlines so powerfully in Psalm 51. David committed adultery with Bathsheba and had her husband killed, and was rightly overcome with conviction for what he had done. Psalm 51 is a great song of deep repentance. After he repents, though, he celebrates his forgiveness, and his newfound right-standing before God. He then pens Psalm 32 as a song to be sung at the annual celebration of the expiation of Israel. This was a time of repentance, and then celebration as the sins of men were carried away from them, never to be seen again. Kind of what communion in church is meant to be like.

David tells us to remember that we are already blessed if our sins are forgiven (vv. 1–2), and they are.

He teaches us that pretending to be righteous is foolishness, as the deceit brings us agony, and God knows anyway and is waiting to forgive us (vv. 3–5). So, we should run to Him as soon as we can, while there is still breath in our lungs, because there is no guarantee of how long that will be true for us (vv. 6–7).

Last, he reminds us that God doesn't forgive and cleanse us begrudgingly, but He does it because He loves us. Our sin does not change that. His love is unfailing, even when we repeatedly fail (vv. 10–11). I love this. He wants to forgive you. He isn't forced into it, and isn't exasperated by having to do it. He loves you! He delights in your return.

That's a stuck record I need to listen to every day of my life.

Prayer:

Father God, thank you that my sins are forgiven—that makes me blessed indeed. Give me faith to celebrate and enjoy your mercy and forgiveness, so that I don't yield to the temptation to be deceitful about my failings. In Jesus's beautiful name, amen.

Psalm 33

Church Music—Turn It Up to 11

Reading:

Take time to read the entire psalm, and then come back to read the following verses again.

> [1] *Shout for joy in the LORD, O you righteous!*
>   *Praise befits the upright.*
> [2] *Give thanks to the LORD with the lyre;*
>   *make melody to him with the harp of ten strings!*
> [3] *Sing to him a new song;*
>   *play skillfully on the strings, with loud shouts.*
>   *Psalm 33:1–3*

Reflection:

I have a long commute most mornings to take my young son Daniel to school. We love to sing in the car together, and we love to sing loud. He likes a band called Coldplay, and when they come on, we have to turn it to 11. It makes me think about how passionately we can sing about things that don't matter, yet we have strange ideas about how we should sing about things that do matter. This psalm (like most of them) is about the collective, about how a group of people should respond to the goodness of God when they are together in a gathering.

So here from Psalm 33 are five suggestions for genuine corporate worship. I hope we embrace them and are found faithful as a people in the way we worship God through music and song in our gatherings.

1. *Righteous folk should be joyful, and they should inform their faces of that fact (v. 1).*

David said that the only people who should sing joyfully are the righteous. The temptation is to think that this only applies to the guys on stage, or to the dude delivering the message, but the glory of the gospel is that it applies to everyone who receives the gift of righteousness from Christ. If you have crossed the line of faith, no matter how you have behaved this week, then that's you. You are the righteous, and the righteous should sing joyfully. The words that David uses here for praise suggest dancing around. Don't be mad—I am just reading the Bible, and the Bible says the righteous should dance around. What intrigues me is that we will do it pretty much everywhere else. We will dance and clap and shout at concerts. We jump up and down at sports games. At church, though, it's like someone put us in quick-set concrete. You are righteous! That's worth celebrating!

2. *Musicians should lead and guide us with instruments that make sense to the culture (v. 2).*

You may be surprised to know that this is a contentious assertion. Most Protestants held the view for centuries that corporate singing should have no instrumentation. David begs to differ. He chooses the harp and the ten-string lyre, and historians tell us that those were the hip instruments of the day. All the best hits that David listened to had a lyre solo just after the bridge. For us, this seems to look like electric guitars and echo pedals. For our kids, it will probably be some dude with an iPad. David says "Hey, whatever instruments stir your hearts and enable you to sing—use those."

3. *We should reflect our creative God by being creative ourselves (v. 3a).*

I love David's exhortation to sing a new song. I think he is telling us to be creative and find new ways to tell God's unchanging story of redemption. This doesn't mean that we kick out old songs. It does mean that we should be writing our own stuff, and even when we sing old songs, we should be doing them in fresh ways that reflect the fresh stirring of our hearts by the gospel.

4. *Bands shouldn't stink (v. 3b).*

It amazes me how in a seeming posture of humility, we just accept junk as acts of worship in God's church. David says that we should practice and be excellent. Somehow the myth has become, "If we get too good, then there will be no room for the Spirit." That's just not right according to the Scriptures. The Spirit of God invented all of those notes and rhythms, and when we use them properly and well, I think we give Him more to work with.

I used to be a full-time musician. I took my craft very seriously. I took it even more seriously when I played in a worship band, as I saw that as my offering of worship to Christ through the ministry of the church. It shouldn't be clinical, but it should be good.

5. *The congregation should get involved (v. 3b).*

David speaks of a give-and-take between the band and the congregation. It's not a show, and so it should never just be people cheering for a band. The vision of the music ministry at our local church is to be the backing band of the congregation. When we, as the congregation, don't sing along, they get sad, and the whole thing becomes a weird facade.

What's your approach to times of music and singing? I pray that we would be a people who worship in spirit and truth. I pray that we would use all means available to create communal experiences of true and joyful worship. Don't stand on the sidelines, saints. Shout for joy! There is a lot to celebrate.

Prayer:

Instead of the prayer today, why don't you turn on some music that turns your heart toward Christ. Sing along, loudly, and acknowledge the goodness of God toward you as you do.

The Goodness of God is Like an Avocado

Reading:

Take time to read the entire psalm, and then come back to read the following verses again.

> ⁶ *This poor man cried, and the L*ORD* heard him*
> *and saved him out of all his troubles.*
> ⁷ *The angel of the L*ORD* encamps*
> *around those who fear him, and delivers them.*
> ⁸ *Oh, taste and see that the L*ORD* is good!*
> *Blessed is the man who takes refuge in him!*
> *Psalm 34:6–8*

Reflection:

For the first fifteen years of my life, I never ate avocados. I just never wanted to try them. They looked a lot more like something that came out of my nose than like something that should go into my mouth. Other people raved about them, but I had no desire to taste them myself. One day, when I was at a good friend's house, avocado toast was the only thing on the lunch menu. His mom refused to serve me anything else and insisted I was being ridiculous for not wanting to eat it. We had it tough as kids.

So, I tried it, and it was amazing. Sweet, and yet tarty. It made the roof of my mouth tingle. I wanted more. I couldn't believe that I had wasted fifteen pre-avocado years simply wondering what it was like. If only I had known how much more meaningful my culinary life could have been if I had included avocados in it earlier.

In Psalm 34, David says that God's goodness is a bit like an avocado. You have to taste it for yourself in order to get it. It is not something reserved for the spiritual elite; in fact, David says that poor men get to experience it. So, while the experiences of others are important, we get to taste of God's goodness ourselves so that we don't just have to take the word of others.

David goes on in the psalm to mention some things about God that we can taste for ourselves.

God listens to and watches the righteous (v. 15), and we get to taste that as we eagerly seek Him out in prayer. When we watch and listen to others pray, we can get an idea of a God who listens, but when we pray ourselves, we get to sense it ourselves.

God ultimately delivers the righteous, in spite of troubles (vv. 17–19), and we get to taste that when we choose to trust Him and praise Him in the most difficult of circumstances.

God is close to the broken-hearted (v. 18), and we get to taste that when we scream out to Him in honest, anguished prayer.

God redeems His servants and doesn't allow them to be condemned (v. 22), and we get to taste that at the communion table. The crunch of the bread tastes like restoration. The bitterness of the wine tastes like forgiveness.

Please don't just believe me on this. Taste and see that the Lord is good for yourself.

Prayer:

Father God, forgive me for the ways where I live off of the spiritual experience of others. Please grant me the faith to try you and trust you myself. Today will provide lots of opportunities to do that. Give me wisdom to see them. In Jesus's name, amen.

Psalm 35

The End of Our Enemy

Reading:

Take time to read the entire psalm, and then come back to read the following verses again.

> [22] *You have seen, O LORD; be not silent!*
> *O LORD, be not far from me!*
> [23] *Awake and rouse yourself for my vindication,*
> *for my cause, my God and my LORD!*
> [24] *Vindicate me, O LORD, my God,*
> *according to your righteousness,*
> *and let them not rejoice over me!*
> [25] *Let them not say in their hearts,*
> *"Aha, our heart's desire!"*
> *Let them not say, "We have swallowed him up."*
> *Psalm 35:22–25*

Reflection:

Some sections of the Psalms can be very difficult to connect with and understand. David is a warrior and soldier, so he speaks naturally and easily of physical enemies and their ongoing desire to kill him with a sword. Here where I live in Johannesburg, while it is known as a pretty hardcore city, it has still been quite a while since someone tried to cut me in half with a sword. In my suburban lifestyle, I am more likely going to go to a day spa than I am to march off into battle.

David is also a sinner, and we need to remember that when we read his poems. So, he hasn't really fully grown in grace to the point where he could always adopt a Christ-like attitude toward his enemies. Jesus told us to love and forgive our earthly enemies (Matt. 5:43–45), but David wants nothing for them except destruction. So, what do we do with Psalm 35? It is still true, inspired, reliable, and authoritative, but it doesn't seem all that helpful for us today. Or does it?

The truth is that we still have a very real enemy who wants to destroy us. You quite simply cannot believe the Bible and not believe in a literal evil one who seeks to destroy mankind and bring us into eternal torment. We haven't done ourselves any favors by being overly obsessed with him, but we commit an equally foolish error when we pretend he doesn't exist. C.S. Lewis said it best when he said,

> There are two equal and opposite errors into which our race can fall about the devils. One is to disbelieve in their existence. The other is to believe, and to feel an excessive and unhealthy interest in them. They themselves are equally pleased by both errors, and hail a materialist or magician with the same delight.[9]

The Bible says that the devil is like a hungry lion, and you are on his desired menu (1 Pet. 5:8). It says that he is a liar and incapable of telling the truth (John 8:44). It says that he loves nothing more than to accuse you day and night and point out your failings all the time (Rev. 12:10).

---

9. C. S. Lewis, *The Screwtape Letters* (New York: HarperCollins, 1941), 3.

So, the next time you fail (which I imagine won't be very long from now), remember that you have an enemy who tempted you to fail. He now stands accusing you, but he cannot be trusted because he is a liar. Remember that one of the great things about the gospel is that it was always foretold that Jesus would destroy Satan (Gen. 3:15), and that Christ has already defeated him on the cross (Col. 2:15). With every passing day, it helps to know that we are one day closer to Christ, and Satan is one day closer to ultimate destruction. When he brings accusation against me, I like to remind him of that fact.

Now, I sound like David. I guess Psalm 35 is useful after all.

Prayer:

Father God, open my eyes to the fact that you have a real enemy who seeks to destroy your people, but open my eyes equally to the fact that you have defeated that enemy, so I don't need to listen to his voice for a moment. In Jesus's victorious name, amen.

Psalm 36

Great Sinner? Great Savior

Reading:

Take time to read the entire psalm, and then come back to read the following verses again.

> ¹ *Transgression speaks to the wicked deep in his heart;*
> *there is no fear of God before his eyes.*
> ² *For he flatters himself in his own eyes*
> *that his iniquity cannot be found out and hated.*
> ³ *The words of his mouth are trouble and deceit;*
> *he has ceased to act wisely and do good.*
> ⁴ *He plots trouble while on his bed;*
> *he sets himself in a way that is not good;*
> *he does not reject evil.*
> ⁵ *Your steadfast love, O LORD, extends to the heavens,*
> *your faithfulness to the clouds.*
> ⁶ *Your righteousness is like the mountains of God;*
> *your judgments are like the great deep;*
> *man and beast you save, O LORD.*
> *Psalm 36:1–6*

Reflection:

There are two ways to read psalms like Psalm 36, that speak of the wicked and their chosen lifestyles. The first way is a moralistic and self-righteous way that says, "Yep, those wicked folk are horrible. They are the real problem with society. We righteous folk should picket and protest, and huddle down together to make sure none of them get in here." This is unfortunately the way many evangelical Christians would read Psalm 36. There is another way, though.

As I read this psalm, bearing in mind the trajectory of all of Scripture that speaks of a good God working in and through a continually rebellious and wicked group of people, I can't help thinking that perhaps the first four verses of Psalm 36 describe people like me. Outside of the grace of God and the substitutionary work of Christ on my behalf, I sound a lot like the man described there. Praise God that my own efforts aren't what I will be judged on, but it is still worth reflecting on what my own efforts look like, because that will save me from self-righteousness.

Left to my own devices, I have no fear of God (v. 1). I flatter myself and seek my own fame all the time (v. 2). Words of deceit often come out of my mouth (v. 3), and I fail to make good and godly decisions regularly (v. 4).

How will a good and righteous God respond to a wicked man like me?

He responds with love that knows no limits (v. 5). He responds by giving me a rock-solid righteousness that cannot be taken away from me (v. 6). He responds by giving me free access to His safe presence (v. 7b). He responds by giving me abundant blessing and joy and delight (v. 8). He responds by giving me life, abundant life (v. 9).

I can't help but think of the wonderful words of John Newton, which he spoke in some of his last days on this earth, after a life well lived. He said, "Although my memory's fading, I remember two things very clearly: I am a great sinner and Christ is a great Savior."[10]

Grace. It's too much.

Prayer:

Father God, I am a great sinner. Teach me to trust in your Son the great Savior.

---

10. John Newton, quoted in John Charles Pollock, *Amazing Grace* (New York: Harper & Row, 1981), 182.

Psalm 37

Kingdom Craving

Reading:

Take time to read the entire psalm, and then come back to read the following verses again.

> ⁷ *Be still before the* LORD *and wait patiently for him;*
>> *fret not yourself over the one who prospers in his way,*
>> *over the man who carries out evil devices!*
> ⁸ *Refrain from anger, and forsake wrath!*
>> *Fret not yourself; it tends only to evil.*
> ⁹ *For the evildoers shall be cut off,*
>> *but those who wait for the* LORD *shall inherit the land.*
> ¹⁰ *In just a little while, the wicked will be no more;*
>> *though you look carefully at his place, he will not be there.*
> ¹¹ *But the meek shall inherit the land*
>> *and delight themselves in abundant peace.*
>> *Psalm 37:7–11*

Reflection:

I like to root for the underdog. We all love a story where the unlikely good guy wins instead of the wicked and evil corporation.

The truth is, though, that the world seems to have very little space for unlikely good guys winning. The "haves" seem to become the "have mores." He who cheats, wins, and those standing up for good and honor and justice usually get trampled on and shut down. It can be totally heartbreaking reading the news and seeing that there seems to be very little justice in the world. If karma rules the universe, then she is broken and cruel.

Psalm 37 has some strange encouragement for us who get so easily frustrated when looking at how the world operates. In essence, it says, "Relax, it won't always be this way. There is a Kingdom coming where the meek inherit the whole thing and the pride-filled are stooped low."

David reminds us that for those who have much in this world through evil means, this is the closest to heaven they will ever get; but for those who seek righteousness, the suffering they experience here is the closest to hell they will ever be.

This is encouragement to endure in a life that seeks the Kingdom of God first, and it is reason to repent for a life that seeks the success of now above all things.

Take heart. It is being fixed. Oh, Lord, hasten the day. Your Kingdom come, on earth as it is in heaven.

Prayer:

Father God, please send your Son soon. Teach us what it means to wait patiently for your Kingdom to come fully and empower us to bring glimpses of it to earth now.

Psalm 38

The Unbearable Burden of Guilt

Reading:

Take time to read the entire psalm, and then come back to read the following verses again.

> *³ There is no soundness in my flesh*
> *because of your indignation;*
> *there is no health in my bones*
> *because of my sin.*
> *⁴ For my iniquities have gone over my head;*
> *like a heavy burden, they are too heavy for me.*
> *Psalm 38:3–4*

Reflection:

Have you ever felt like this? Have you ever been sick to your stomach at your own sin? Have you ever been so overwhelmed by your guilt that you felt like you couldn't take it, and you wondered how you would be able to continue? Ever wondered how long God might endure your rebellion?

David felt it.

Psalm 38 is difficult to read. David was in deep anguish because of his sin. This is far from the "live with no regrets," self-help thinking of today. David had deep regrets, and he was a man after God's own heart, we are told (Acts 13:22).

So, in Scripture it seems that it is good and right for our own sin to grieve us. We need to be familiar with our own fallen state. It is part of our humanness, and mustn't be denied or glossed over.

But that is half the picture, because as familiar as David is with his fallen condition, he is equally familiar with the faithfulness and mercy of his Savior God. Psalm 38 laments for a long time about sin, but then it finishes by rejoicing in the certainty of God's salvation.

> ¹⁵ But for you, O Lord, do I wait;
>   it is you, O Lord my God, who will answer...
> ²¹ Do not forsake me, O Lord!
>   O my God, be not far from me!
> ²² Make haste to help me,
>   O Lord, my salvation!

So, know your sin. Let it grieve you as it should. Some of us don't take our sin seriously enough. In prayer today, confess your sin openly before God. Let it grieve you. Name it. Bring it into the light.

But please, know your Savior, and your source of salvation, and let Him meet you in your broken state, with mercy, grace, love, and restoration.

As committed as we are to rebellion, He is to salvation.

Prayer:

Father God, forgive me for the ways I gloss over sin and make it seem as if it isn't a big deal. It is. Teach me to grieve over sin, and teach me equally to trust in the mercy you offer for a sinner like me.

Psalm 39

The Wisdom of Living Like You're Dying

Reading:

Take time to read the entire psalm, and then come back to read the following verses again.

> *⁴ "O Lord, make me know my end*
> *and what is the measure of my days;*
> *let me know how fleeting I am!*
> *⁵ Behold, you have made my days a few handbreadths,*
> *and my lifetime is as nothing before you.*
> *Surely all mankind stands as a mere breath! Selah*
> *⁶ Surely a man goes about as a shadow!*
> *Surely for nothing they are in turmoil;*
> *man heaps up wealth and does not know who will gather!"*
> *Psalm 39:4–6*

Reflection:

It is one of the rare and special privileges of my job that I get to stand with families on their worst day. I don't enjoy it by any stretch of the imagination, but every time I get to stand with a family at the side of the grave of a loved one, I feel especially privileged.

The privilege isn't just that a family would trust me to speak words of comfort at that occasion, but the privilege is also that God would lovingly remind me of the fact that all mortal men meet a common end. It is a strange blessing to be reminded of that fact, because in our foolishness, we often forget. In fact, Solomon said that we get more out of the reminders that come from funerals than we do out of our best parties.

> It is better to go to the house of mourning than to go to
> the house of feasting, for this is the end of all mankind,
> and the living will lay it to heart (Ecc. 7:2).

David didn't want to forget his mortality, so in Psalm 39 he cried out to God in prayer, asking God to remind him how short his life here on earth is. Why would he do such a thing? Was he morosely fascinated with death? Was he suicidal? I don't think so.

I think that David knew, as we all know, that men who know they are dying usually live differently. They tend to focus on the things that matter for eternity, and as David so poignantly reminds us in verse 6, stuff that we accumulate doesn't matter for eternity.

So, here is the reminder for today.

You are going to die.

It is good for you to know that. Every breath you take is one less breath until your loved ones stand around your grave while they lower you into the ground.

Make it count. Live for stuff that lasts.

Maybe spend some time reflecting on what you want your legacy to be, and make some commitments to live toward that with the days you have left.

Prayer:

Father God, teach me to know just how fleeting I am, and teach me to let that knowledge change the way I live with the days I have left.

Psalm 40

"Sing This with Me—This Is 40"

Reading:

Take time to read the entire psalm, and then come back to read the following verses again.

> ¹ *I waited patiently for the* Lord*;*
> *he inclined to me and heard my cry.*
> ² *He drew me up from the pit of destruction,*
> *out of the miry bog,*
> *and set my feet upon a rock,*
> *making my steps secure.*
> ³ *He put a new song in my mouth,*
> *a song of praise to our God.*
> *Many will see and fear,*
> *and put their trust in the* Lord*.*
> *Psalm 40:1–3*

Reflection:

I grew up in a house with two older brothers. This meant that most things in my early life were dictated to me, rather than decided by me, but my brothers did choose some things for me that I am grateful for to this day. One of them was my taste in music. I listened to whatever my brothers listened to, and for the most part that was a very good thing. My oldest brother did have a weird obsession with Chris De Burg and even Erasure at one point, but he has repented of that season, and has faithfully returned to Springsteen, Sting, REM, and other real bands.

One of my favorite memories of hanging out with my brothers, though, was when we lay on our beds and listened to U2's magnificent *Under a Blood Red Sky* album. Three boys, transfixed by the magnificence of a live performance, all singing along as if we were there. They made us believe anything was possible. One song on that album stood out from the rest. It was just called "40," and it grabbed my soul. The words were taken straight from Psalm 40, and the Scripture resonated with me deeply. David was telling his own story of faith. I loved that he had a personal journey with the Creator of the universe. He could speak of that journey, and it mattered. It mattered enough for it to go in the Bible. I wanted to be able to speak of a personal journey with my God one day, too.

Now I can.

Much like David, I know what it feels like to wait for the Lord. His timing and mine don't seem to work off the same clock, and there have been long seasons in my life when I have wondered what He was up to, or if He was even still there.

Much like David, I can testify that He always answers, and He always pulls me up out of the mud and mire I have gotten myself into.

Much like David, I can boldly say that He gives me a safe and firm place to stand through His truth and grace. I continually find ways to step off of that and sink back into the mud, but time and time again He puts me back on the rock of His truth.

Much like David, He has changed my heart to such an extent that I feel I have a new song of praise in my mouth.

And much like David, my desire is that many would see and hear through me of His goodness, grace, and beauty. That is my deepest prayer.

What's your story of God's faithfulness?

It matters. It's your new song, and it should be shared. Are you in a season of waiting? Hang in there and know that He hears and will come get you. Are you stuck in the mud and mire? Cry out to Him, and He will clean you off and stand you back on solid ground. But don't pretend like you are cool when the mud is up to your nostrils.

Take some time today to reflect on what God has done for you. Thank Him.

Prayer:

Father God, teach us to be people who wait more patiently for you and for the way you always work things for our good. Put a song of praise in my mouth so that others might know how good you are.

Psalm 41

Downside Up

Reading:

Take time to read the entire psalm, and then come back to reflect on the following verses.

> *¹ Blessed is the one who considers the poor!*
>   *In the day of trouble the LORD delivers him;*
> *² the LORD protects him and keeps him alive;*
>   *he is called blessed in the land;*
>   *you do not give him up to the will of his enemies.*
>   *Psalm 41:1–2*

Reflection:

In 1876, Spurgeon said in a sermon,

> I think you may judge of a man's character by the persons whose affection he seeks. If you find a man seeking only the affection of those who are great, depend upon it he is ambitious and self-seeking; but when you observe that a man seeks the affection of

those who can do nothing for him, but for whom he must do everything, you know that he is not seeking himself, but that pure benevolence sways his heart.[11]

This was later simplified in 1972 by Malcolm Forbes, who said,

You can easily judge the character of a man by how he treats those who can do nothing for him.[12]

The meditation today then will simply be a question that has been plaguing me since I read Psalm 41. In a culture and society that lords and applauds only the strong and successful, what can I do today for the weak? What can I do today for someone who can do nothing for me in return?

This is by no means an add-on to the gospel. When we fully understand that we are the weak who can do nothing in return to repay God's goodness, grace, and mercy toward us, then it is a logical extension for us to reach out to the weak.

The Kingdom of God is downside up. The weak will be strong; those who mourn will rejoice. Reach out today to someone who needs reaching out. The Kingdom of God will come near.

Prayer:

Father God, thank you that you reached out to me in my weakness. I had no ability to help myself, but you saved me. Give me eyes to see those all around me who need help that I could reach out to as a response to that great gospel. In Jesus's name, amen.

---

11. Spurgeon, *Metropolitan Tabernacle Pulpit: Sermons Preached and Revised During the Year 1876, Volume XXII* (Pasadena, TX: Pilgrim Publications, 1981), 373.
12. Malcolm Forbes, *The Sayings of Chairman Malcolm: The Capitalist's Handbook* (New York: HarperCollins, 1978).

SELAH POINT 1

Instead of rushing off into the next book straight away, take some time to think back and reflect on what God has been teaching you through the last forty-one devotions. Take out a piece of paper or journal, and ask the Holy Spirit to help you capture some of the big lessons you have been learning in the Psalms.

Take your time, press in, pause. Selah.

BOOK TWO
(42 – 72)

Wherever the Psalter is abandoned, an incomparable treasure vanishes from the Christian church. With its recovery will come unsuspected power.

— *Dietrich Bonhoeffer*

Yea, the Psalter...might well be entitled a Little Bible, wherein everything contained in the entire Bible is beautifully and briefly comprehended, and compacted into an enchiridion or Manual... the Psalter is the very paragon of books.

— *Martin Luther*

Psalm 42

Family Ties

Reading:

Take time to read the entire psalm, and then come back to read the following verses again.

To the choirmaster. A Maskil of the Sons of Korah.

> [1] *As a deer pants for flowing streams,*
>   *so pants my soul for you, O God.*
> [2] *My soul thirsts for God,*
>   *for the living God.*
> *When shall I come and appear before God?*
>   *Psalm 42:1–2*

Reflection:

The Psalms shift at Psalm 42, like a chapter in a book or an act in a play, and for the first time we are formally introduced as readers to some other contributors. To be fair, many people still feel that David wrote Psalm 42, and that the "Sons of Korah" were just the chosen performers of the piece; but even if that is the case, these men are obviously very important when it comes to the corporate worship Israel was participating in.

That can seem like superfluous information, but the Scripture is very meticulous and doesn't often waste words. Why would it bother to tell us that the Sons of Korah wrote this piece or that they needed to perform it?

One of the reasons is to teach us that there are different gifts for the people of God. The Sons of Korah didn't sing like crows, so they got to do the singing. Being musicians, they were probably terrible at admin, so they had someone else do that. I love how God equips His body with different gifts, and people should operate in their areas of strength for the building up of the body.

One of the other reasons, I think, is that the Sons of Korah had a checkered family history. Korah had questioned God's selection of Moses and Aaron as leaders and had led a rebellion against them, proposing himself and others as alternative leadership (Numbers 16). God wasn't pleased, apparently, so He killed Korah and his mates by swallowing them up with the ground, which must have been a terrifying sight. But I love how God works His slow, redemptive purposes through generations. The Sons of Korah weren't cursed forever by the sins of their forefathers, but ended up playing a key role in God's redemptive move through Israel.

Their storyline had changed. God had intervened, and redeemed.

So, what does your family story look like? God can still intervene and change it. You don't have to be like your forefathers. You also can't catch godliness from them. Korah came from the line of Levi, but that lineage didn't make Him a godly guy. At some point, the sons of Korah decided to follow God with passion and purpose. They longed for Him and sought Him first above all things.

You can do the same, even if you don't have a good past. You must do the same, even if you do have a good past. Seek him now, in this moment.

Prayer:

Father God, thank you that we don't have to be defined by the sins of our forefathers. Thank you for grace. Thank you for new beginnings. Help us make the most of those things in our generation and be people who long for you.

Psalm 43

Moody Blues

Reading:

Take time to read the entire psalm, and then come back and re-read the following verse.

> *Why are you cast down, O my soul,*
> *and why are you in turmoil within me?*
> *Hope in God; for I shall again praise him,*
> *my salvation and my God.*
> *Psalm 43:5*

Reflection:

I struggle with my moods. I always have. I tend to waver between being elated and pretty pumped up about stuff, to being quite despondent and downcast. It isn't a total rollercoaster of emotion, but it also isn't plain sailing with "Captain Consistent" by any stretch of the imagination.

A problem can creep in when we believe the caricature that evangelical Christianity has created of itself. In order to be a Christ follower, it would seem that one is expected to be consistently chipper and chirpy. Ned Flanders from *The Simpsons* is funny as a character because he so cleverly mocks what we have created as a sub-culture.

Then, there is the Bible, and the Bible is full of moody folks who do their best to love God and follow Him. Church history is jam-packed full of difficult people who sometimes experience long and dark nights of the soul. It would seem I am in good company in my occasional gloominess.

Psalm 43 gives us the cure to the blues, though. The solution to being downcast isn't to look further inward to figure it out there. In fact, the harder I examine my own dysfunction, the more cause for gloom and despair I have. The solution, according to the Psalmist, is to remember where hope lies. Hope lies in the unchanging nature of God.

When I remember He is eternal, then what I am facing today seems temporal and insignificant, and that brings me joy. When I remember He is unchanging, then my faithless despair is trumped by His faithful grace, love, and mercy, and that brings me comfort. When I remember He is sovereign, then even the largest obstacles in my life seem like they won't destroy me, and that brings me hope. When I remember that He is loving enough toward me to have sent His Son to pay the price for my sin, then my rebellion, or even my obedience, doesn't define me; but I am defined by the immovable righteousness of Christ, which cannot be revoked. That gives me courage.

Are you downcast? That's okay. Hope in God.

Prayer:

Father God, when I am downcast I choose to hope in you and believe in your faithfulness. Remind me God, again and again, of how good you have been to me, so that I don't give in to the tyrannies of my moods. In Jesus's name, amen.

Psalm 44

The Olden Days

Reading:

Take time to read the entire psalm, and then come back to read the following verse again.

> *O God, we have heard with our ears,*
> *our fathers have told us,*
> *what deeds you performed in their days,*
> *in the days of old.*
> *Psalm 44:1*

Reflection:

I enjoy studying history. It has been said that the past has a habit of repeating itself, so a person who is a student of the past could also be said to be someone who is best equipped to understand and survive the future. I have taken this to heart when it comes to church, so I have found myself to be a keen student of church history. I love to read books by and about dead guys. I find them the most interesting, and usually the most insightful. It is tremendously encouraging to hear the stories of what God did in the generations that went before us. Stories of transformed lives, renewed societies, and changed cities. Stories of revival. Stories of God's greatness. Stories of ordinary people with extraordinary faith and belief.

But God hasn't changed. Sure, He chooses to work in some generations and locations differently from others, but why wouldn't He work in ours?

My prayer is that my great-grandchildren would be able to identify with Psalm 44:1. I pray that they will hear of a great God who does great things. I pray that their dads will love Jesus, and their dads will tell them of the great things God did in the generation of their great-grandpa. Then I pray that they will love God, and live in such a way that their great-grandchildren can say the same thing.

You've got one life here on earth. What do you want your generation to be remembered for? I want ours to be remembered for the great things God did among us, so we must do all we can to live faithfully for Him.

How will your life be remembered? Will you be remembered as someone who was radically faithful to God and who experienced His hand at work in your day and age?

Prayer:

Father God, teach us to live for a multi-generational legacy of faithfulness so that our great-grandchildren could hear about the incredible things you did in our midst.

Psalm 45

If You Like It, Then You Better Put a Ring On It

Reading:

Take time to read the entire psalm, and then come back to read the following verses.

> ^{7b} *Therefore God, your God, has anointed you*
> *with the oil of gladness beyond your companions;*
> ⁸ *your robes are all fragrant with myrrh and aloes and cassia.*
> *From ivory palaces stringed instruments make you glad;*
> ⁹ *daughters of kings are among your ladies of honor;*
> *at your right hand stands the queen in gold of Ophir.*
> ¹⁰ *Hear, O daughter, and consider, and incline your ear:*
> *forget your people and your father's house,*
> ¹¹ *and the king will desire your beauty.*
> *Since he is your* LORD, *bow to him.*
> ¹² *The people of Tyre will seek your favor with gifts,*
> *the richest of the people.*
> *Psalm 45:7b–12*

Reflection:

Psalm 45 is a psalm about a wedding. It speaks about a gorgeous bride who is nervous, excited, and elated all at once. It speaks about a handsome groom who is strong and brave, dressed in his best on his finest day. It says some strange things about the bridegroom, though. It says he is blessed forever. It says he is robed in majesty and splendor. It says he displays awesome deeds. It says that nations fall beneath his feet, and it says he will reign forever. Now, I have done a lot of weddings, and this doesn't describe any of the grooms I have seen. They usually just look surprised and terrified. Some historians think that this psalm described the wedding between Solomon and Pharaoh's daughter, but even the splendor of that day could never be said to equate with what is being described in Psalm 45.

Psalm 45 has always been thought by scholars and commentators to be Messianic. It is quoted by the writer of Hebrews in reference to Christ's work (Heb. 1:8). It describes Christ as the groom and His church as the bride, just as Paul goes on to describe Christ's commitment to the church in Ephesians. This is language that is often quite difficult for men to understand, but it is magnificent when we think through the implications.

As the groom, Jesus's love for us is proactive. This is no leap year arrangement where we ask Him, He proposes to us, and He wins us over through His grace and love.

As the groom, Jesus's love for us is permanent. When He enters a covenant, He keeps it. I love that Jesus doesn't date us, or live with us, or flirt with us. He is in covenant with his bride the church, regardless of how we treat Him.

As the groom, Jesus's love for us is passionate. Ephesians tells us that He gave himself up for us. He lays it all on the line, and He spares nothing in winning us to Himself.

As the groom, Jesus's love for us is purifying. His holiness cleanses us so that we can stand confident, looking our best, dressed in white as a bride on her wedding day. We just get to do it every day.

Jesus is the groom, and the bride is us—His church. That is great news.

Prayer:

Father God, thank you that you have given your church as a bride to your beloved Son, to be united to Him forever. Thank you for the covenant commitment that your Son displays toward us. We wait for Him, Lord.

Psalm 46

God Is

Reading:

Take time to read the entire psalm, and then come back to read the following verses again.

> *¹ God is our refuge and strength,*
>> *a very present help in trouble.*
> *² Therefore we will not fear though the earth gives way,*
>> *though the mountains be moved into the heart of the sea,*
> *³ though its waters roar and foam,*
>> *though the mountains tremble at its swelling. Selah*
>>>> *Psalm 46:1–3*

Reflection:

What does your mind run to when there is trouble about? Many of us love to play out various scenarios and eventualities, and as we do so the size and scope of our travails get bigger and more fearful, and our anxiety increases. It can end up feeling like the earth beneath us is giving way, and there doesn't seem to be any way out.

In the midst of strife, the Psalmist doesn't start that way. He starts abruptly with, "God is." I love the certainty of that. He takes the certainty of God's character to the difficult circumstances of the people, and instead of those problems growing, they shrink.

Why? God is.

God is our refuge and our strength. He is the one we can run to in order to find shelter, and He is the one who fights for His people to keep our attackers at bay. God is a very present help. What a thought! He is very present, right here, available and loving.

God is!

Later on in this psalm, God says to restless human hearts, "Be still, and know that I am God" (v. 10a). Do you know who God is? You can run to Him.

Prayer:

Father God, give us greater confidence in who you are, and let that confidence drive us to greater faith and confidence in you. Forgive us for the times we aren't still and sure in the knowledge of who you are. Help us, Lord. You are who you say you are.

Psalm 47

Be a "Happy Clappy." It's Biblical.

Reading:

Take time to read the entire psalm, and then come to read the following verses again.

> *¹ Clap your hands, all you nations;*
>   *shout to God with cries of joy.*
> *² For the LORD Most High is awesome,*
>   *the great King over all the earth.*
> *³ He subdued nations under us,*
>   *peoples under our feet.*
> *⁴ He chose our inheritance for us,*
>   *the pride of Jacob, whom he loved.*
>   *Psalm 47:1–4*

Reflection:

I grew up in churches. I saw most different types of expressions of them as a young man, and I was utterly convinced that the crazy folk who seemed to enjoy times of corporate singing and gathering were flat out wrong and a little creepy. Now, a lot of that had to do with the fact that those folks also tended to take four special anointing offerings to pay for the apostle's teeth whitening, but that aside; I was also persuaded that their expression of worship was wrong. We had it right, I thought. We were miserable, and that's biblical...isn't it?

Well, the truth is that if you aren't particularly fond of physically expressive corporate worship, you will probably hate the Psalms, or you may have to read them with a "Tippex" pen to remove all the uncomfortable parts about the "happy-clappies." They are all over the place in the Psalms. Even worse than that, psalms like Psalm 47 are said to be prophetic, with this particular one talking about the return of Christ and our eternal worship of Him. So, we will worship Him joyfully and expressively one day.

What about today?

We have seen throughout the Psalms that we don't have to pretend with our moods, and we don't have to just make out that everything is okay. This psalm, then, isn't a call to a mono-emotional Christian experience. It is saying that when we consider the fact that God is King over all the earth, it should drive joy out of us; otherwise, we aren't truly believing it.

When was the last time you clapped your hands and shouted songs of joy to your God? If it has been a long time, it has probably been a long time since you properly considered His wonderful kingship over you and over the peoples of the earth.

Do that now. Lift your head. Raise your voice. Clap your hands.

God is King.

Prayer:

Father God, forgive me for the times when I have displayed an indifferent response to your goodness, majesty, and kindness toward us. Teach me to respond in faith and to be enthusiastic and full of fervor in my praise of you.

Psalm 48

God Is Older Than You

Reading:

Take time to read the entire psalm, and then come back to read the following verses again.

> [12] *Walk about Zion, go around her,*
> *number her towers,*
> [13] *consider well her ramparts,*
> *go through her citadels,*
> *that you may tell the next generation*
> [14] *that this is God,*
> *our God forever and ever.*
> *He will guide us forever.*
> *Psalm 48:12–14*

Reflection:

I have started to really like old people. They have peculiarities, to be sure, but I love hanging out with folks who have lived significantly longer than I have. They have a wisdom that I have yet to develop, that comes from experiencing a wealth of things I am yet to experience. They also know that they don't have long left, so they tend to say whatever is on their mind. If more young folks would just shut up and listen to the old folks a bit more, the world would be a far smarter and altogether kinder place. I sound like the old folk now, but it's true.

The Bible tells us repeatedly that God is eternal. My brain can't even begin to grapple with the fullness of the implications of that, but by my calculations that makes Him much older than I am, and much older than everyone. He has quite simply seen it all. But it gets even better, because eternity runs forward, too, and that means He isn't aging, and He isn't past his best. He is just the same. Forever. And He will always be around. He isn't going anywhere.

For some people, this is a major obstacle to faith, but to me it is one of the most glorious truths in the world. It means that whatever I am going through, God has seen it before, and He is able to be a reliable guide for me, filled with the wisdom and knowledge I so desperately need.

So, what about you? What temporal situation do you have that could use some eternal wisdom? Does your situation seem hopeless? God has seen millions of people overcome suffering and struggle, and He has personally redeemed hopeless looking people into world changers. Don't give up—He hasn't.

Does your situation seem endless? God has seen how it plays out, and He knows what lies on the other side of it. Find some hope in Him.

Does your situation seem final? God is in the business of resurrecting the dead. It isn't over 'til He says it's over.

Prayer:

Father God, you have always been and will forever be. Teach us to submit to your wisdom and holiness, and to run to you in our limited understanding.

Psalm 49

He Who Dies with the Most, Loses

Reading:

Psalm 49 is so rich in wisdom, and literally every line is golden. Read it slowly, and then come back to read the following verses again.

> *7 Truly no man can ransom another,*
> *or give to God the price of his life,*
> *8 for the ransom of their life is costly*
> *and can never suffice,*
> *9 that he should live on forever*
> *and never see the pit.*
> *Psalm 49:7–9*

Reflection:

In a world where systems are built around the notion of simply acquiring more and more and more until you die, and where those who have acquired the most, or have the appearance of having acquired the most, are lauded as heroes, Psalm 49 cuts right against the grain and exposes the futility and folly of wealth as the basis for identity, worth, and joy.

No matter how much wealth one acquires, it will never be enough to save you from death (vv. 7–9). The same fate befalls the rich and the poor (vv. 10–11). Nobody is super impressed by the guy with the fanciest tombstone.

It is quite sobering.

The answer, then, is not to be poor and to find identity in that, but to look to the One who can save you from death and find your identity, worth, and joy in Him.

Jesus is abundantly rich, but made Himself poor to come and redeem us. Everyone gets put in the grave, but not everyone will walk out of it into eternal riches. The promise of eternal reward with Christ is a certain identity that won't fail us. That's why the Scripture can tell us not to build up treasures here on earth, but rather to build it in heaven, where it is secure.

Ask the Lord to show you the ways you are living purely for the folly of now. You may find that the temporal things you are fighting to own are simultaneously fighting to own you. None of those things will go with you when you are gone.

Prayer:

Father God, forgive us for the thousands of ways we build up treasures on earth instead of banking on the certainty of heaven. Teach us to trust you and live as thankful and ransomed people.

Psalm 50

Ridiculous Religion

Reading:

Take time to read the entire psalm, and then come back to read the following verses again.

> 7 *"Hear, O my people, and I will speak;*
> *O Israel, I will testify against you.*
> *I am God, your God.*
> 8 *Not for your sacrifices do I rebuke you;*
> *your burnt offerings are continually before me.*
> 9 *I will not accept a bull from your house*
> *or goats from your folds.*
> 10 *For every beast of the forest is mine,*
> *the cattle on a thousand hills.*
> 11 *I know all the birds of the hills,*
> *and all that moves in the field is mine.*
> 12 *"If I were hungry, I would not tell you,*
> *for the world and its fullness are mine.*
> 13 *Do I eat the flesh of bulls*
> *or drink the blood of goats?*

¹⁴ Offer to God a sacrifice of thanksgiving,
and perform your vows to the Most High,
¹⁵ and call upon me in the day of trouble;
I will deliver you, and you shall glorify me."
Psalm 50:7–15

Reflection:

Psalm 50 is one of those passages of Scripture that should make us all really uncomfortable. It's a "big God, little me" reminder, and we tend to resist those. God is reminding Israel of their place in the grand scheme of things, and He is lovingly remonstrating with them to not forget where they fit in that grand scheme. Israel had fallen into the trap that all of us religious people fall into. We think that we pull the strings and God dances to our tune. As if we are good and therefore He must respond in kind. We make sacrifices, and He should feel good about that.

The problem with that is it makes it seem like God is trying to please us. It makes it seem as if God desperately needs us, when He really doesn't. He owns it all. It is all for His good pleasure. When we give stuff to Him, we are really giving His stuff back to Him, and we do it to remind us of that fact—not to impress Him.

Some will think that this truth makes God seem cruel. I personally love it, because this is the God that sacrificed so much to pursue us through His Son. He didn't do it because He needs us, but because He loves us and desires to see us live for His glorious name. That is more amazing than a God who needs us. It also totally eliminates karma and religious effort. We obey God not to try and please a cosmic scorekeeper, or to tip the scales of goodness our way. We obey Him because we understand that we are totally possessed by Him. We are His, and that is glorious.

BIG GOD, LITTLE ME!

So be thankful, be faithful, be humble, and be joyful.

Prayer:

Father God, give us a real sense of your size, majesty, and holiness. Help us see that we are creatures designed to worship and serve you, and that doesn't diminish our value or purpose, but rather enhances it. Teach us to live for you, Lord!

Psalm 51

Real Repentance

Reading:

Take time to read the entire psalm, and then come back to read the following verses again.

> [10] *Create in me a clean heart, O God,*
> *and renew a right spirit within me.*
> [11] *Cast me not away from your presence,*
> *and take not your Holy Spirit from me.*
> [12] *Restore to me the joy of your salvation,*
> *and uphold me with a willing spirit.*
> *Psalm 51:10–12*

Reflection:

Psalm 51 has to be one of the most gut-wrenching passages in all of Scripture. It was written by David after he had been confronted by the prophet Nathan about his adultery with Bathsheba and his murder of her husband. David was rightly horrified by what he had done, and he penned Psalm 51 as an act of repentance.

Repentance is a word used often at church, so we can forget to stop and look at what it really means. In David's painful song, we have a great model of biblical, real repentance.

Real repentance requires an understanding of the nature of God (v. 1). David started by remembering God's unfailing love and great compassion. If we don't believe that God loves us, and if we don't believe He has enduring compassion toward us, then we won't want to approach Him with our sin. On the other hand, if we do believe that He is loving and compassionate, then we can't wait to run to Him, knowing full well how He will respond.

Real repentance requires an understanding of the nature of our sin (v. 3). David was honest about his sin and he didn't try to mask it, cover over it, or make it seem less offensive and horrific. He looked at it long and hard, and confessed it fully. If God knows the fullness of our sin anyway, and if that doesn't alter His nature or His determination to be loving and merciful toward us, then there is no reason for us to walk in secrecy and pretense.

Real repentance requires an understanding of the nature of God's restoration (v. 7, vv. 10–12). David knew that God could cleanse him fully from his past sin, and he knew that God could also transform his heart so that he could be more able to stand against temptation in the future. If God loves us enough to restore us, instead of just begrudgingly forgiving us, we should be quick to go to him with our dysfunction, and quick to cry out to him for restoration.

Real repentance requires humility (v. 17). David was broken before God. Admitting failure is by default a humbling position, and real repentance can only come from a humble heart that is crying out, "I can't do this. I need you."

Real repentance leads to joy (v. 12). David's sin had led to misery, but he prayed that his repentance would lead to a restoration of joy. We keep believing that sin will lead to joy and repentance will lead to misery, but the opposite is true. When we practice real repentance, we furiously pursue our own joy.

Martin Luther reminded us that Jesus willed the entire life of believers to be one of repentance. What do you have to repent of today? I hope that Psalm 51 will help you do it in a real and biblical way, and I hope that it will bring you much joy.

Prayer:

Spend some time repenting of your sin and celebrating your Savior in prayer.

Psalm 52

Tongue Tied

Reading:

Read the entire psalm and then re-read the following verses.

> *² Your tongue plots destruction,*
> *like a sharp razor, you worker of deceit.*
> *³ You love evil more than good,*
> *and lying more than speaking what is right. Selah*
> *⁴ You love all words that devour,*
> *O deceitful tongue.*
> *Psalm 52:2–4*

Reflection:

Psalm 52 is about a guy called Doeg the Edomite. He had a catchy name, and he also had a loose tongue. He chose to further Saul's suspicion of David by sharing rumors of his whereabouts, which ended up in the slaughter of a whole family of priests as Saul acted off of Doeg's information.

There were consequences to Doeg's words. There always are consequences to words. "Sticks and stones will break my bones, but words will never harm me," is just not true.

The Bible speaks repeatedly about the power of words and about the danger of a tongue that speaks them without thinking. David says that a tongue can be like a sharpened razor, cutting and tearing and damaging. He says that falsehood is harmful, that it hurts and destroys.

So here are some useful questions for you to ponder next time before you share a piece of information.

Is it true?

Are these the real facts or have they been embellished, even a little, to make me look better, or to make them look worse, or to make the whole situation seem to be a little more dramatic than it really is?

Is it worshipful?

Sometimes, things are true but they aren't things you would want to say if Jesus were in the room. They aren't things that grow your heart in affection toward Him. This question keeps me silent quite often, and that's a good thing.

Would I say it if the person were here?

I am trying to live my life in a way that says stuff to people and not about people. I am far from successful in this, but I am finding that I live with way less guilt and I inflict way less damage if I decide not to say anything about you I wouldn't be prepared to say to you.

Does it build up, or break down?

It is easy to break someone down. I discovered early on that I am particularly good at it, and have used it as a defense mechanism for years. It is far tougher to build someone up in a meaningful way. If it breaks down, then hesitate to speak; and if it builds up, don't hesitate at all. Just say it.

Let us be people who are slow to speak, and as a result let us be people who don't inflict pain with our words.

Prayer:

Father God, forgive me for the many ways that I use words to inflict harm on others. Teach me to instead use my mouth for your glory and for the building up of others. Teach me to speak truth and put away falsehood. In Jesus's name, amen.

Psalm 53

Hopeful Hindsight

Reading:

Read the entire psalm, and then come back to read the following verses again.

> *² God looks down from heaven*
> *   on the children of man*
> *to see if there are any who understand,*
> *   who seek after God.*
> *³ They have all fallen away;*
> *   together they have become corrupt;*
> *there is none who does good,*
> *   not even one.*
> *Psalm 53:2–3*

Reflection:

For the most part, Psalm 53 seems and looks hopeless. It contains a sentiment that I think a lot of us can identify with sometimes. When I look at the world, I can find myself agreeing with David that everyone has turned away and together become corrupt. No one seems to do good. Especially not me. It seems hopeless. Who will redeem us and change this thing up?

David was looking forward to a future hope, though. Someone would rise up out of Zion and bring back hope to a hopeless people.

> Oh, that salvation for Israel would come out of Zion!
> When God restores the fortunes of his people,
> let Jacob rejoice, let Israel be glad.
> Psalm 53:6

Oh, how grateful I am that what David looked forward to has already happened. Jesus rose up out of Zion, and He is restoring the fortunes of His people! As a result, the people of God can once again rejoice and be glad.

Some days, I still feel hopeless. What I need to do, then, is look back at the fact that salvation came out of Zion, and that one day Jesus is returning.

Let's rejoice and be glad. David never got to see it, but we know of the great Savior from Zion.

Prayer:

Oh, Lord, when I look at the world, it can seem as if everyone has turned their back on you. But thank you, Father, that you raised hope from out of Zion. There was one who obeyed perfectly, and in Him we find hope. It is in His mighty name we pray, amen.

Psalm 54

Being Sure When You Aren't Sure

Reading:

Take time to read the entire psalm, and then come back to read the following verses.

> *³ For strangers have risen against me;*
> *ruthless men seek my life;*
> *they do not set God before themselves. Selah*
> *⁴ Behold, God is my helper;*
> *the LORD is the upholder of my life.*
> *Psalm 54:3–4*

Reflection:

Psalm 54 is yet another Psalm where David finds himself in deep trouble. It's something of a repeat theme. I am totally baffled as to how people can believe the kind of theology that says following God will result in a trouble-free existence. Didn't Jesus say something about that?

I have told you these things, so that in me you may have peace. In this world you will have trouble. But take heart! I have overcome the world .

John 16:33 NIV

Jesus clearly says that His followers will run into all sorts of trouble and strife. The good news doesn't keep them from that. The good news declares that He is significantly better than anything they will encounter, and that He will never abandon them regardless of what they are facing.

David had real trouble. Lots of people were trying to kill him. He didn't make light of his circumstances or water them down at all. He didn't pretend like they didn't exist. He did, however, remember to be certain about the nature of God in the face of trouble.

He said, "Behold," as if he were sure, even when he wasn't. None of his circumstances led to "behold," yet he chose to believe it.

What are you facing? Do you have trouble? The key to joy and faith is not to pretend like you aren't facing problems, but rather to be sure when your circumstances are unsure.

Behold, God is our helper.

Prayer:

Father God, forgive us for the times that we allow our circumstances to cloud our knowledge of your goodness. Give us the faith to behold your goodness even and especially on days when we cannot see it.

Psalm 55

Me Time

Reading:

Take time to read the entire psalm, and then come back to read the following verses again.

> ¹⁶ *But I call to God,*
>   *and the* LORD *will save me.*
> ¹⁷ *Evening and morning and at noon*
>   *I utter my complaint and moan,*
>   *and he hears my voice.*
> ¹⁸ *He redeems my soul in safety*
>   *from the battle that I wage,*
>   *for many are arrayed against me.*
>   *Psalm 55:16–18*

Reflection:

We live in the most connected era in human history. At the touch of a button, or the flick of a switch, we have access to information from across the planet. We are able to interact instantly with a multitude of people, some we know, and many we don't.

It's a beautiful privilege if you think about it. We really should do more productive things with that access. The danger in this increased connectivity, though, is two-fold. First, we can forget to communicate well with the people who are right in front of us. Have a look around at restaurants and check out the families sitting across the table from each other, looking at their phones. I really want my family to see my face a lot more than they see the back of my iPhone.

The second danger, and the one I want to talk about, is that we run the risk of watching other people's lives more than we do our own. We look on longingly when other people succeed. This is true even in our spiritual journey, as we can now connect with Christian "rock star" pastors and authors. We hope to catch some of their spiritual superstardom from them, but they seem to operate in a different realm. This connectivity should bless us, but it can actually leave us feeling despondent and disheartened. How do these guys get to know God in a way that seems impossible for me?

We can also look on confounded at all the bad news in the world. The news reports are continual, repetitive, and detailed, and every horrible failing of humanity is highlighted in a way that it never has been before. This can leave us discouraged and desperate as people of faith. Lord, who will fix all of this?

In Psalm 55, David spends a lot of time looking at other people. How could they be so wicked? How could they be so powerful?

When he is focusing on the fate of others, he seems pretty hopeless, but then the tone of the psalm shifts. He starts talking about the faithfulness of God in verse 16. As a logical consequence of reflecting on God's nature, David stops worrying about others too much and how they are doing, and stops and examines himself for a bit.

Maybe today, take some time to think about you. Not in a selfish way, but in a realistic and honest, self-assessment way. For a moment, stop looking over other's fences and stop worrying about what others think and what motivates them. Just focus on you and God.

Can you say with David,
But I will trust in you?
I hope so.

Prayer:

Father God, forgive me for spending so much time gazing into the lives of others, usually in a covetous fashion. Teach me to be content with my own life and to examine my own heart and faithfulness before you.

Psalm 56

Fear Fighting

Reading:

Read the entire psalm, and then come back to reflect on the following verse.

> *When I am afraid,*
> > *I put my trust in you.*
> > > Psalm 56:3

Reflection:

I have some utterly irrational fears.

I am scared of sharks. That doesn't sound all that irrational, but I am truly scared of sharks in any body of water. The pool at the gym, for instance, is not a place you would find me swimming. I could probably win Olympic gold in a swimming event. As soon as I hit the water, I become convinced I am about to get eaten from behind. It's a horrible and crippling thought.

I am scared of spiders. Like, properly scared. Like, "I won't enter a room with a rain spider in it" scared (rain spiders are large but harmless spiders common in South African homes). All of my deepest complementarian convictions evaporate the second one of those suckers enters our house, and my wife Sue has to become the head of the household—and fast. It makes very little sense to be so scared of something that can't harm you.

But I also have more, seemingly rational, fears.

What if I lost someone I loved?
What if my children rebelled and walked away from God and our family?
What if I got sick?
What if I failed in ministry?
What if Jesus grew tired of me?

Sometimes, these things make me afraid. The beauty of Scripture is that there is room for fear in our human existence. It is assumed by David in Psalm 56:

When I am afraid...

I love what comes next, though. David doesn't try to minimize his fear, but he doesn't dwell on his fear, either. He acknowledges it and meets it with faith. The Scripture says that faith is being certain of what we do not see (Heb. 11:1). That implies we have to go through fear to faith, and without the fear it doesn't take faith.

So, what are you afraid of? Own it. Own up to it.

Then, fight it with faith.

Prayer:

Father God, teach me to have more fear of you and less fear of anything else that I encounter. In Jesus's name, amen.

Psalm 57

The Great Barista in the Sky

Reading:

Take time to read the entire psalm, and then re-read the following verses.

> [7] *My heart is steadfast, O God,*
> *my heart is steadfast!*
> *I will sing and make melody!*
> [8] *Awake, my glory!*
> *Awake, O harp and lyre!*
> *I will awake the dawn!*
>   *Psalm 57:7–8*

Reflection:

I was in line to order a coffee not long ago at one of my favorite coffee spots in the city. I am a pretty simple coffee order kind of guy. Cappuccino. Sometimes, a skinny if I am having a fat day, but it doesn't really get more complex than that for me. The person in front of me ordered a decaf, soy, honey and almond latte, with cinnamon sprinkle. That level of pretense or decaffeinated complexity shouldn't be allowed.

It got me thinking, though. We live in a very "custom" age. We can trick anything out so that we can always have something just the way we like it. From cuts of jeans, to specs on cars, everything can be made to tickle our particular desire and fancy. It has made us into quite a demanding people, actually—people whose needs need to be met, because that is what we are used to.

We have brought this attitude into our worship of God, and even into our general attitude toward God. If He does what I think He should do, He gets worship. When we gather, if the band plays a particular style at a particular volume, then you will have my attention.

David isn't getting a custom God when he writes Psalm 57. In fact, nothing is working out the way he would have liked. He was living in exile in a cave. It wasn't what he ordered.

His response was incredible, though. He didn't wait for God to impress him toward worship. He didn't wait until he felt like it. He decided he would sing truth whether he felt like it or not. He made a determination to sing and make music about the goodness of God.

Are you perhaps in danger of treating God like your barista in the sky? Are you waiting for Him to conjure up just the right custom mix for you before you are moved to praise and serve Him? Or will you, like David, make a determination to worship?

Prayer:

Father God, forgive me for testing your goodness by placing it within the confines of my customized view of how you should be good to me. Teach me to be more steadfast and committed to praising you for who you are and not just for what I think you should provide for me.

Psalm 58 & 59

Strange but True

Reading:

Take the time to read both Psalm 58 and Psalm 59, and then come back to reflect on the following verses. Disclaimer: the reading today isn't comfortable at all.

> *⁶ O God, break the teeth in their mouths;*
> *tear out the fangs of the young lions, O LORD!*
> *⁷ Let them vanish like water that runs away;*
> *when he aims his arrows, let them be blunted.*
> *⁸ Let them be like the snail that dissolves into slime,*
> *like the stillborn child who never sees the sun.*
> *Psalm 58:6–8*

Reflection:

Psalm 58 and Psalm 59 are so similar in theme and tone that I decided to lump them together into one meditation. This gives you an off day tomorrow, and you may well need it.

The Bible makes me really uncomfortable. It's a wild book, and it makes no apologies for that. Ironically, that is part of what makes me trust it so much. It isn't full of niceties and platitudes that are of little or no use in the real world. It doesn't cover up the horrendous and horrific things people do. Even people who are prominent in the story think and say terrible things, and they are recorded in the Scriptures for all to see. I really appreciate that.

Spurgeon said, "Defend the Bible? I would sooner defend a lion. Simply open its cage and let it out and it will fend for itself."[13]

Psalms 58 and 59 have a repeat theme, and they have had me flummoxed for days. Is it okay for a preacher to say that? I really don't know what to do with them.

David was undergoing a great deal of persecution from his enemies, but his response to them was not particularly gracious. He wanted God to knock their teeth out. And he wanted things that are way worse than that to befall them, too.

So here are a few learnings I took away from Psalms 58 and 59 that encouraged me. I am still not sure what to do with the rest. I don't doubt them to be true and helpful; I just don't fully understand them yet.

I hope these thoughts encourage you, too.

1. The Bible is mysterious, and that shouldn't detract from its truth. In fact, in order for it to be true, it should be mysterious. Its mysterious nature makes me want to read it more, not less.

2. God loves people with major issues. David is a man with a deep desire for vengeance, and God loves him. Passionately, relentlessly, and selflessly.

3. Human leaders have been terrible from the beginning, and they will be terrible until Jesus brings this thing to a close. When David describes the injustice of the rulers of his day, my heart cries out that there is nothing new in the world. That makes me strangely hopeful.

---

13. Spurgeon, "The Lover Of God's Law Filled With Peace," The Metropolitan Tabernacle, Newington, January 22, 1888.

Prayer:

Father God, thank you that there are strange and difficult words recorded in the Scriptures for our good. Thank you that there is space for human frailty. Teach me to trust your Word.

Psalm 60

This Hurts Me More Than It Hurts You

Reading:

Read the entire psalm, and then come back to read the following verses again.

> ^{1} *O God, you have rejected us, broken our defenses;*
>   *you have been angry; oh, restore us.*
> ^{2} *You have made the land to quake; you have torn it open;*
>   *repair its breaches, for it totters.*
> ^{3} *You have made your people see hard things;*
>   *you have given us wine to drink that made us stagger.*
>   *Psalm 60:1–3*

Reflection:

My son Daniel is starting to get to the age where we will need to begin thoughtfully disciplining him. He understands enough of what we are communicating, so we are going to need to start addressing his rebellion (common to all people) in order to lovingly grow him, teach him, train him, and protect him.

It is a tough thing for parents to do. I never enjoy it. I never thought through how tough it must have been for my parents to discipline me.

I assumed they loved sending me to the bathroom, which was the spot they chose for me to go for a time of isolation and contemplation. It was a weird room to pick, but it was effective.

Psalm 60 is a painful song about God's discipline. He had told His people repeatedly that their rebellion would ultimately have consequences, and that He would use surrounding nations to discipline them and bring them back to Himself.

Then He did it, and it was as terrible as everyone expected.

Discipline, though, is supposed to strengthen relationships and not weaken them. It is supposed to bring the "discipliner" and "disciplinee" closer together and not push them further apart. It is supposed to restore and not destroy.

The trouble comes in when we perceive any kind of discipline as rejection instead of as a loving, corrective hand from an adoring parent. The Scripture says time and time again that God will lovingly discipline His kids. It even says that this is a sure sign He loves us and that He hasn't left us as orphans. We should be worried if we don't experience discipline.

How are we responding when God does intervene?

If you think you may be undergoing the discipline of the Lord, are you running toward Him or away from Him? Are you experiencing this season as evidence of His love, or are you feeling rejected by Him?

Can you cry out in urgency like David,

You have been angry; oh, restore us!

I pray that we can.

Prayer:

Father God, thank you for your immense patience with compulsive rebels like us. Teach us to trust you in tough seasons, and teach us to run to you and not away from you in those seasons. Do what you need to do as a loving Dad to change us and grow us. In your Son's name we pray, amen.

Psalm 61

Likeness and Otherness

Reading:

Take time to read the entire psalm, and then come back to re-read the following verses.

> *¹ Hear my cry, O God,*
> *listen to my prayer;*
> *² from the end of the earth I call to you*
> *when my heart is faint.*
> *Lead me to the rock*
> *that is higher than I,*
> *³ for you have been my refuge,*
> *a strong tower against the enemy.*
> *Psalm 61:1–3*

Reflection:

One of the great mysteries of Christianity, that I believe makes it more hopeful than any other system of beliefs or ideologies, is the incarnation of Jesus. God became a man and came to the world to rescue His creation. In doing so, He allowed himself to have a fully human experience in which He felt pain, despair, joy, temptation, fatigue, cold, heat, hunger, feasting, laughter, and pretty much anything else you can think of, except sin. It is a wonderful thing to get your head around.

God knows how you feel. He felt it, too.

But equally important to remember is that God is holy and completely unlike us, so we don't get to focus on the God who knows human experience without also acknowledging that He isn't in any way restricted by humanity's limitations. He is still God.

His power is without reserve. Now, He doesn't experience fatigue or discouragement or limitation. That makes the incarnation even more remarkable—that such a great God would be so kind is remarkable.

Sometimes, we forget the tension and see God just as a peer-type figure. A therapist who dishes out helpful sayings, but isn't really able to help us, even if he can identify with us. Psalm 61 helpfully shatters that idea for us.

David knew he needed someone not like him to save him. He grew faint, and he needed someone who never grows faint. He was overcome by his enemies, and he needed someone who never gets overcome. He was a mere man, and he needed a strong tower, a rock that couldn't be moved, and a refuge where he could be safe. He found all of those things in the sovereign God.

Whatever you may be facing today, remember that you have a God who sympathizes with your weaknesses, but please also remember that you have a God who is not restricted as you are. You need someone who is like you to love you, but you need someone who is not like you to fix you.

Jesus can do that.

Prayer:

Father God, thank you that you sent your Son into the world. He is our sympathetic High Priest, and He understands our weaknesses. Thank you also that you aren't constrained by our weaknesses and are able to rule in all circumstances. Give us faith to trust you and humility to obey you.

Psalm 62

It's Not Up to Me

Reading:

Take time to read the entire psalm, and then read the following verses again.

> [7] *On God rests my salvation and my glory;*
> *my mighty rock, my refuge is God.*
> [8] *Trust in him at all times, O people;*
> *pour out your heart before him;*
> *God is a refuge for us. Selah*
> *Psalm 62:7–8*

Reflection:

I trusted Christ for salvation when I was seven years old. I knelt at the foot of my parents' bed, and my dad knelt with me as I confessed that I was a great sinner who needed a great Savior. I knew that I needed the righteousness of Christ to put me into right standing with God.

The problem was that then I believed the lie that said staying in right standing with God depended on me. "Jesus got me in, but I will keep me in," was the way that my twisted thinking defaulted toward. The problem with this was that I continued to be a rebel, so it seemed to me all the time that my salvation was tenuous, and that as I found new ways to rebel, God would ultimately tire of me and cut me loose. This was a terrifying thought that led to lots of guilt, lots of bargaining with God, and lots of pretending to be better than I really was.

Passages like Psalm 62 are really helpful to tired religious souls like mine who are sometimes tempted to try to keep their salvation by being good.

On God rests my salvation and my glory.

Wow, God gets me in, and God keeps me in. My salvation is a result of His divine will and work, and He gets to decide on my righteousness based on His Son. So, even when I don't act like the redeemed son that I am, I still am a redeemed son because the work of redemption depends on God and not on me, and God doesn't fail like I do. This is something worth shouting from the rooftops. God gives salvation. My salvation depends on Him!

This is brilliant news for someone who knows that they will fail. My hope isn't in me. My hope is in God. Thomans Le Blanc once said of this verse:

> On the shields of the Greeks, Neptune was depicted; on the shields of the Trojans, Minerva; because in them they put their confidence, and in their protection deemed themselves secure....Now, Christ is the insignia of our shields.[14]

Where is your hope for salvation being placed? I pray that it is in Christ. Carry that shield with His name on it, and nothing can take you down.

---

14. Thomans Le Blanc, quoted in Spurgeon, *The Treasury of David, Volume 2*, 56.

Prayer:

Father God, thank you so much that my salvation rests on you. Teach me to rest and delight in that truth and to serve you all the more faithfully because of it.

Psalm 63

Thoroughly Thirsty

Reading:

Take time to read the entire psalm, and then read the following verses again.

> *¹ O God, you are my God; earnestly I seek you;*
>   *my soul thirsts for you;*
>   *my flesh faints for you,*
>   *as in a dry and weary land where there is no water.*
> *² So I have looked upon you in the sanctuary,*
>   *beholding your power and glory.*
> *³ Because your steadfast love is better than life,*
>   *my lips will praise you.*
> *⁴ So I will bless you as long as I live;*
>   *in your name I will lift up my hands.*
>   *Psalm 63:1–4*

Reflection:

A friend of mine who is struggling in their walk with God asked me the other day if I ever feel like I am disconnected from God, or if pastors always just walk closely with Jesus.

I laughed, out loud, for quite a long time. The truth is that large parts of my journey in pursuit of Christ have felt like I have been wandering in the wilderness with no clear direction, and no obvious divine companion.

Prayers often feel unanswered, even when I know they are answered.

The Bible can feel unbelievable and even uninspired, even though I know full well it is both believable and inspired.

God can feel far away, even when I know He hasn't moved.

Psalm 63 was written by David when he found himself in a literal wilderness. He had been chased from the city by his son Absalom, and he was thirsting to death in the cruel desert wilderness. I love how he responded, though. He didn't try to pretend as if he weren't where he was. He didn't make up grand imagery of an oasis filled with waterfalls. He also didn't give up on God or allow his understanding of who God is to be clouded by his difficult circumstances, and he didn't try to ignore God or sulk because he had been seemingly abandoned.

David declared the truth of God's nature in the wilderness. He called him both *Elohim* and *Eli*. One is plural and one is singular. He is God over all and He is God over me. David acknowledged in the midst of his hardship that God was still God over everything as sovereign Lord and King, but David also remembered that God was loving and personal and interested in David as an individual. David kept on seeking God in the wilderness. David didn't give up or give in, but earnestly sought the Lord. He realized in his thirst and weakness that God was absolutely essential for everything. He knew that God wasn't an add-on in his life, but that He was as essential as life-giving water.

So, some questions for you.

Do you find yourself in the wilderness spiritually? How will you respond in that season? Will you curse God and bemoan where you are? Or will you, like David, take time to acknowledge who God is, and will you pursue Him for all you are worth, realizing that you need Him more than anything?

Prayer:

O God, you are my God; earnestly I seek you; my soul thirsts for you; my flesh faints for you, as in a dry and weary land where there is no water. Amen.

Psalm 64

Who Are You Listening to?

Reading:

Take time to read the entire psalm, and read the following verse again.

> *Let the righteous one rejoice in the L*ORD
> *and take refuge in him!*
> *Let all the upright in heart exult!*
>   *Psalm 64:10*

Reflection:

As you get older, you start to realize some really interesting things about yourself. You realize that you weren't that smart when you were younger, and you realize that while you may be smarter now, you certainly aren't as good-looking, energetic, or hip. You also learn, incidentally, that you were never that hip in the first place.

You learn more serious and difficult things about yourself and your personality, core things about you that you never knew were there. One of those core things I have realized recently is that I have spent most of my life desperately desiring the approval of others. I want other people to adore me, and I want it all the time. It's a bitter curse, to be honest, and it hounds me fairly consistently. The ridiculous thing is that everyone feels it, and so everyone walks around fighting for the approval of the other, and we all assume that the other person in our relationships holds the power because they can bestow or withhold approval. Meanwhile, they are looking back at us assuming we have the power. It's so foolish and fickle.

Psalm 64 strongly juxtaposes two avenues for self-assessment. One is in the words of others. It is fickle and precarious, and it hurts like mad when they say things about us that we don't like.

> ³ They sharpen their tongues like swords
>   and aim their words like deadly arrows.
> ⁴ They shoot from ambush at the innocent man;
>   they shoot at him suddenly, without fear.
>   Psalm 64:3–4 (NIV)

The other avenue is described as a refuge. A safe place where there is certainty. Where you are declared righteous, no matter what people may say about you. Where you are declared loved regardless of how you have performed. Where you are declared fearfully and wonderfully made, because the one declaring it is the one who made you.

> Let the righteous rejoice in the LORD
>   and take refuge in him;
>   let all the upright in heart praise him!
>   Psalm 64:10

Where will you go for your understanding of worth? Will you go to those who are actually trying to play the same self-worth game and who will put you down to lift themselves up, albeit ever so briefly? Or will you go to the One who made you, the One who redeemed you, the One who loves you, and the One who desires to be with you?

I know which one I prefer.

Prayer:

Father God, forgive me for the wasted effort and energy of allowing the words of others to determine my sense of worth and purpose in the world. Teach me to be someone who hears clearly from you and who trusts in your unfailing love to give me a sense of humble security and identity.

Psalm 65

At My Worst, God Gives His Best

Reading:

Take time to read the entire psalm, and then read the following verse again.

> *When iniquities prevail against me,*
> *you atone for our transgressions.*
> *Psalm 65:3*

Reflection:

One of the strangest things we have associated with Christianity is guilt. In fact, many Christians seem to wear guilt as some kind of badge of honor and holiness. It comes from flawed thinking that suggests that the guiltier I feel over my failures, the more pleased God must be. If I am truly miserable for a long time, then God must be delighted. What it does is place me right back at the center of earning my own salvation. This thinking seems to suggest that the depth of my guilt is directly proportional to my right standing with God.

Psalm 65 talks about being overwhelmed with deep guilt because of sin and rebellion. It is a feeling most of us know well. It then tells us how God meets us when we are in this place. The NIV is helpful here:

> When we were overwhelmed by sins,
> you forgave our transgressions.
> Psalm 65:3 (NIV)

Just think about that for a second. He doesn't kick us when we are down. He doesn't take great joy in some prolonged moping. He sees us straining under guilt and removes it from us. How good is that?

I love how Eugene Peterson captured verses 2 through 4 in the Message:

> We all arrive at your doorstep sooner
> or later, loaded with guilt,
> Our sins too much for us—
> but you get rid of them once and for all.
> Psalm 65:2-4 (MSG)

When you are convicted of your sin, repent. That is a good and appropriate response. But then remember to rest in the knowledge that God forgives you through Christ and doesn't desire for you to labor under your guilt any longer. He paid a great price so that you could experience joy and not further bondage.

Prayer:

Father God, thank you so much for the mercy and forgiveness you offer us through your Son. When I am overwhelmed, you forgive. Help me believe that.

Psalm 66

Deal or No Deal?

Reading:

Take time to read the entire psalm, and then come back to read the following verses again.

> *¹³ I will come into your house with burnt offerings;*
> *I will perform my vows to you,*
> *¹⁴ that which my lips uttered*
> *and my mouth promised when I was in trouble.*
>   *Psalm 66:13–14*

Reflection:

I have made lots of deals with God. They usually happen when I am in trouble of some sort. I have made promises to never drink again when a teenage me found myself in a rapidly spinning room, if only God would make the space stop spinning. I have made promises to be a brilliant scholar for the rest of my life when I found myself walking up to a results board at university, if only God saw to it that I passed. I have made promises to be a missionary to go wherever God wanted me to go, if only God made sure that my friends' parents never told my parents what we were up to on the weekend. I have made promises to give my life to service of the Lord forever, if only God would spare my dad long enough for me to take my flight across the Indian Ocean so that I could see him alive one more time.

All of these promises were made, and all of these deals were brokered, when I was in moments of crisis. Suffering and discipline have a real way of focusing our lens so that we remember what is important. The problem is that we tend to forget all of these when things go well. We needed God terribly when we were in trouble, but then all too quickly return to our misplaced confidence in self.

In Psalm 66, the Psalmist outlines his history of walking with God. He recalls the great times of walking in comfort, and he also recalls the really tough times of crisis, and times when he was being disciplined by God. In those days, he made some vows to God. He got through those tough days, though, and returned to smoother terrain, but he remembered the vows that he made and was intent on seeing them through.

My question to you today is, will you fulfill the vows you made?

Will you follow Christ and show your total dependence on Him in good times and bad? Or will it take another crisis to get you to your knees?

> When you make a vow to God, do not delay to fulfill it. He has no pleasure in fools; fulfill your vow. It is better not to make a vow than to make one and not fulfill it.
>
> Ecclesiastes 5:4–5 (NIV)

Prayer:

Father God, forgive me for the many ways that I have turned my back on my commitment to you and to your ways. Thank you that you remain relentlessly committed. You always keep your promises. Help me, by the power of your Holy Spirit, to obey you.

Psalm 67

Glad Nations

Reading:

Take time to read the entire psalm, and then read the following verses again.

> *¹ May God be gracious to us and bless us*
>> *and make his face to shine upon us, Selah*
> *² that your way may be known on earth,*
>> *your saving power among all nations.*
> *³ Let the peoples praise you, O God;*
>> *let all the peoples praise you!*
>
> *⁴ Let the nations be glad and sing for joy,*
>> *for you judge the peoples with equity*
>> *and guide the nations upon earth. Selah*
> *⁵ Let the peoples praise you, O God;*
>> *let all the peoples praise you!*
>>> *Psalm 67:1–5*

Reflection:

I am a blessed man indeed. God is so good to me, and as I examine my life, it is so obvious to me that I don't deserve what I have. Everywhere I look is evidence of God's blessing and grace. Even the tough stuff in my life just screams out His renown. That's really why it is all there. It is all there to shout out about Him. It is there so that everyone will see Him.

This is exactly what Psalm 67 is getting at. It starts with a prayer for blessing, but quickly turns to the point of blessing. The point is so that everyone in every nation would know of His salvation.

So today is a really brief exhortation. What are you doing with the blessing that you have been given? Before you ask for more, ask yourself how you are using what you have for the glory and fame of the One who blessed you.

Whom will you tell of His goodness today? Who will hear of His salvation from you today? If the nations are going to be glad, then the people of God will need to declare the goodness of God to them.

The news is too good not to share.

Prayer:

Father God, thank you for the thousands of ways you have displayed your goodness toward me. Give me opportunity and courage to speak of that goodness to others, so that your way may be known on the earth.

Psalm 68

Burden-Bearing God

Reading:

Take time to read the entire psalm, and then read the following verses
again.

> [19] *Blessed be the* L ORD,
>   *who daily bears us up;*
>   *God is our salvation. Selah*
> [20] *Our God is a God of salvation,*
>   *and to* GOD, *the* L ORD, *belong deliverances from death.*
>
> *Psalm 68:19–20*

Reflection:

Just four brief thoughts from Psalm 68 to hopefully encourage you.

First, God is with us in our suffering. Verse 19 says that He bears
us up when we are burdened. This sets the God of the Bible apart
from any other deity or worldview. He is a compassionate God who is
with us in suffering. The incarnation of Jesus was the ultimate evidence
and validation of that. I love the thought that when I feel like I am
struggling under a heavy load, God bears me up.

Second, He doesn't abandon us for periods in our suffering. Sometimes, it can feel like we are walking the dark parts of the journey on our own, but the Psalmist confidently declares that He bears our burdens daily. This points to a God who is involved in the detail of our lives. This speaks of a God who perseveres with us in our pain. This speaks of a God who never leaves.

Third, He is sovereign even over suffering. When we recognize from the Scripture that God is compassionate toward us, we sometimes can't help but picture Him as bemused, and confounded by suffering, just like us. The Psalmist is quick to remind us, though, that He is a sovereign God of salvation who oversees everything, and has power and authority over everything, even death.

Last, this incredible God who is with us, and never abandons us, and rules over the universe, also cares for us in our struggles and pain. He isn't cool and unfeeling. 1 Peter 5:7 says,

> Cast all your anxieties on him, because he cares for you.

He is with you.
He will never leave you.
He has power over how it plays out.
He cares for you.

Prayer:

Heavenly Father, there is nothing unknown to you and nothing you cannot use for my good and your glory. Help me trust you more in the circumstances of my life.

Psalm 69

Man of Sorrows

Reading:

Take time to read the entire psalm, slowly. It is painful and heart-breaking. Then come back and read the following verses again.

> ^{19} *You know my reproach,*
> *and my shame and my dishonor;*
> *my foes are all known to you.*
> ^{20} *Reproaches have broken my heart,*
> *so that I am in despair.*
> *I looked for pity, but there was none,*
> *and for comforters, but I found none.*
> ^{21} *They gave me poison for food,*
> *and for my thirst they gave me sour wine to drink.*
> *Psalm 69:19–21*

Reflection:

Psalm 69 is quoted seven different times in the New Testament. It appears that the writers of the New Testament believed that this particular psalm spoke not only of the sorrows, struggles, heartache, and pain of David, but more importantly of the sorrows, struggles, heartache, and pain of the new and better David, who is Jesus. It is amazing to consider that the pain David felt over his own sin pointed to the pain Christ was going to feel over the sins of the world that would be placed upon Him.

He was scorned when He deserved to be praised.
He was disgraced when He deserved worship and adoration.
He was shamed when He deserved to be exalted.
His heart was broken when He deserved unbridled joy.
He was left to look helpless, when He deserved the throne of ultimate authority.
He was given no sympathy, even as He was saving those who wouldn't give it to Him.
He was left uncomforted while He was fulfilling His promise to bear the burdens of the world.
They put vinegar in His wine, while He bled for their sins.

I am continually astonished by the depths that Jesus went to in order to win my salvation. We should never grow familiar with it. When I forget it, I can quickly become discontent with my own lot, but when I remember what Christ has done, my satisfaction levels with what I have, and the path that I have been given, rise.

As St. John of the Cross said, "Whenever anything disagreeable or displeasing happens to you, remember Christ crucified and be silent."

When the cross of Christ is clearly pictured in my mind, I find it almost impossible to doubt God's good intentions toward me, regardless of my circumstances.

Prayer:

Father God, when I think of the sufferings of your Son in my stead, I am grieved over the sins that made His sacrifice necessary. Help me soberly reflect on your mercy and live a new life secure in the knowledge of the lengths you went to in order to redeem us.

Psalm 70

I Dare You to Move

Reading:

Take time to read the entire psalm, and then read the following verses again.

> *⁴ May all who seek you*
> > *rejoice and be glad in you!*
> > *May those who love your salvation*
> > *say evermore, "God is great!"*
> *⁵ But I am poor and needy;*
> > *hasten to me, O God!*
> > *You are my help and my deliverer;*
> > *O LORD, do not delay!*
> > > *Psalm 70:4–5*

Reflection:

Psalm 70 is a rollercoaster of emotion. It speaks graphically of what it is like to have enemies who taunt you and remind you of your failings. It speaks of feeling lost and hopeless and full of despair. Then, it switches in verse 4 and speaks boldly of what it is like to be seeking God and experiencing the joy of the salvation He brings. It speaks of worshipping and exalting God even when times are tough. This is part of why I love the Psalms so much. The writers are as up and down as so many of us are.

I love what the psalm does in verse 5, though. It honestly declares that the Psalmist isn't really feeling up to verse 4 at that time. It's true that the righteous rejoice and are glad because of God's salvation. It's true that they exalt God. Yet, the writer feels poor and needy and distanced from God.

How does he respond in that space? Does he hide himself from God and skulk away, knowing that he hasn't lived up to what the righteous are supposed to do? No, he cries out all the more for God to come to his aid quickly. He knows that he isn't where he wants to be with God, and that sends him running straight to God instead of away from Him.

So how are you doing in your journey? Do verses like verse 4 irritate you because you know you aren't there? How do you respond to that? Many of us then hide from God and His influence, because we are ashamed of where we are and how we might be received. Don't be like that. Be like David. Cry out from where you are for God to meet with you, and quickly.

I love what John Newton said when he so eloquently assessed himself:

> I am not what I ought to be—I am not what I wish to be —I am not what I hope to be. Yet, though I am not what I ought to be, nor what I wish to be, nor what I hope to be, I can truly say, I am not what I once was.[15]

So, by all means, be honest about where you are, but also look back at where God has brought you from, and run quickly to Him again.

---

15. John Newton, quoted in Joseph Foulkes Winks, ed., *The Christian Pioneer* (Glasgow: 1856), 84.

Prayer:

Father God, thank you that you don't give up on us regardless of how close to you we feel. I pray that we would be people who are quick to run to you and to trust in you when we fall.

Psalm 71

Finishing Strong

Reading:

Take time to read the entire psalm, and then read the following verses again.

> *⁵ For you, O LORD, are my hope,*
> *   my trust, O LORD, from my youth.*
> *⁶ Upon you I have leaned from before my birth;*
> *   you are he who took me from my mother's womb.*
> *   My praise is continually of you.*
> *⁷ I have been as a portent to many,*
> *   but you are my strong refuge.*
> *⁸ My mouth is filled with your praise,*
> *   and with your glory all the day.*
> *⁹ Do not cast me off in the time of old age;*
> *   forsake me not when my strength is spent.*
> *   Psalm 71:5–9*

Reflection:

A few weird things have happened to me as I have approached my late thirties. I have started watching what I eat, as I can no longer eat exactly what I want without pronounced midriff consequences. I have started heading home from functions early, as I can no longer rip it up 'til late at night without long recovery periods; and, besides, I can't stand the music these kids are listening to.

But more than these superficial things, I have noticed something way more serious and interesting. As I have come to the point where I have been out of school longer than I was in it, I have started to look back on my life in reflection on how well I have done, and I have started to look forward to that inevitable day when my time will be up. I now wonder what I will have accomplished come that fateful day.

This is normal, I am told, and it gets worse in your forties, and your fifties, and so on, until you stop caring or breathing, whichever comes first. This is why so many people have to hype up and overplay what their youth was like. We need "Glory Days" to make it seem like our life has counted. This is also why people have mid-life crisis incidents, as we try to make sure our remaining days are jam-packed with joy, activity, and meaning.

In Psalm 71, the Psalmist is looking back on his life and his walk with God. He declared boldly that he had followed and obeyed God since his youth. What a great thing to be able to say. But he was worried that he would stray in his old age and that he wouldn't finish well. What a sad fate that would have been.

My own journey with Christ has been a mixed one. I can't say I have relentlessly pursued God from my youth. I wandered from the path many times as a young man. My path has meandered and drifted, and it has been dark and muddled at times.

I know what I want my future to be like, though. I want to be worshipping God when I have grey hair and massive ears. I want to lift my hands up off my walker and wave them in the air in praise of my great King.

Jesus said that once we taste the goodness of the gospel, we should follow him resolutely for the rest of our lives. In a very tough passage in Luke 9:62, he said:

> "No one who puts his hand to the plough and looks back is fit for service in the kingdom of God."

I can't change my past. I can reflect on it, and, as a result, I can put my hand to the plough and make a determination to not look back. That's what I am doing. This is my prayer, and my promise.

> Even when I am old and gray,
>   do not forsake me, O God,
> till I declare your power to the next generation,
>   your might to all who are to come.
>   Psalm 71:18 (NIV)

Prayer:

Father God, forgive me for the time that I have wasted chasing things and not following you. Help me spend the rest of my years more faithfully.

Psalm 72

The King is Dead.
Long Live the King!

Reading:

Read the entire psalm and then read the following verses again.

> ¹ *Give the king your justice, O God,*
> *and your righteousness to the royal son!*
> ² *May he judge your people with righteousness,*
> *and your poor with justice!*
> ³ *Let the mountains bear prosperity for the people,*
> *and the hills, in righteousness!*
> ⁴ *May he defend the cause of the poor of the people,*
> *give deliverance to the children of the needy,*
> *and crush the oppressor!*
> *Psalm 72:1–4*

Reflection:

There seems to be something of a leadership crisis in the world today. All of the great nations of the earth are scratching their heads and wondering where the next great statesman will come from. In South Africa (where I live), people are growing increasingly discontent with the gap between the promises our government has offered, and what has actually been delivered to the people, especially the poor.

Who will lead us out of the mess we are in?

In Psalm 72, David had reached the end of his reign as king. Most commentators agree that his son Solomon penned it, but that David spoke it, probably from his death bed. It is a prayer from a dying king. A prayer for a new kind of king. A just king. A merciful king. A kind king. A loving king. A loyal king. An honest king.

It is pretty obvious that he isn't praying for Solomon, though. He is praying for a king that will rule as long as the sun. He is praying for the King of Kings.

I, like David, pray for the final rule of that King. I can't wait.In the meantime, I get to partner with Him in pointing to His Kingdom. When Jesus prayed, "Thy kingdom come, Thy will be done, on earth as it is in heaven," He was telling us that every time we do the will of the King, the Kingdom comes on earth.

Christians, instead of spending all of your energies hoping for justice from an earthly leader, why not spend some energy bringing the Kingdom to earth, so that when Jesus returns as King, many recognize him because they have felt and seen his Kingdom come near them through you? Ask God to help you manifest the Kingdom in your sphere of influence—to live more justly, kindly, empathetically, and wisely where you are for the good of others and the glory of God's name.

Prayer:

Father God, please don't delay in sending your Son to fully establish your Kingdom. In the meantime, though, please change the hearts of the kings of earth, and please empower your church to live as citizens of the Kingdom to come.

SELAH POINT 2

In the Psalms so far, you have been exposed to some of the most earnest and passionate prayers ever recorded. Before moving on to the next book, why don't you take some time today to spend in earnest prayer? Get yourself a quiet spot, write down some things you would like to pray about, and refuse to move on until you feel like you have communed with God. Wrestle through the distractions, make sure you are away from technology, and spend longer than you usually would. Enjoy some communion with your Father, who loves to hear your requests.

BOOK THREE
(73 – 89)

The psalms, like no other literature, lift us to a position where we can commune with God, capturing a sense of the greatness of his kingdom and a sense of what living with him for eternity will be like.

— Gordon Fee

The Psalms are honest: there is no easy triumphalism and no attempt to disguise the trials that beset believers.

— G.W. Grogan

Psalm 73

Joburg vs. Heaven

Reading:

Read the entire psalm, and then read the following verses again.

> ² *But as for me, my feet had almost stumbled,*
> *my steps had nearly slipped.*
> ³ *For I was envious of the arrogant*
> *when I saw the prosperity of the wicked.*
> ⁴ *For they have no pangs until death;*
> *their bodies are fat and sleek.*
> ⁵ *They are not in trouble as others are;*
> *they are not stricken like the rest of mankind.*
> Psalm 73:2-5

Reflection:

I live and minister in a very status-driven context. Our church community is situated in the Northern Suburbs of Johannesburg, and while it might surprise some readers to know this, it is a place driven by status and the appearance of wealth. Friends who visit us from overseas cannot believe how much we are prepared to spend on cars. The same applies to clothes, watches, phones, and even houses. We want to show everyone that we have "made it," even if we haven't.

We are the perfect example of those who spend money we don't have, to buy things we don't need, to impress people we don't even like. It creates a massive pressure that can leave people deeply discontent about their own circumstances when everyone else seems to be doing so well.

Psalm 73 speaks of the dangers of a life lived trying to measure up to the successes of those around us who appear to have more than we do. It leads to despondency, envy, and a victim mentality as we bemoan the fact that we don't have what others have.

The solution the Psalmist offers up is to consider what you have in light of eternity.

> [25] Whom have I in heaven but you?
>> And there is nothing on earth that I desire
>> besides you.
> [26] My flesh and my heart may fail,
>> but God is the strength of my heart and my
>> portion forever.
>
> Psalm 73:25–26

My wife Sue and I are busy considering some lifestyle changes, but as we do that we are being careful to ask ourselves two questions. First, are we making some attempt to impress others around us from an envy-driven motive? Second, will these changes matter for eternity, and do they make sense in light of heaven?

I find it very difficult to be discontent with what I have when I think of heaven. But I find it very difficult to be content with what I have when I think I have to live up to a standard set by the appearances of people around me.

Prayer:

Father God, teach me to be content with what I have. Teach me to stop comparing myself to others and to look to heaven, and to desire nothing so much as I desire you.

Psalm 74

Autumn and the Greatness of God

Reading:

Read the entire psalm, and then read the following verses again.

> ¹⁶ *Yours is the day, yours also the night;*
> *you have established the heavenly lights and the sun.*
> ¹⁷ *You have fixed all the boundaries of the earth;*
> *you have made summer and winter.*
> *Psalm 74:16–17*

Reflection:

Psalm 74 is a lament. It is a sad assessment from the Psalmist of the seeming lack of the work of God that he has seen in his own generation. It quite possibly was written in response to the Babylonian destruction of Jerusalem, so the situation that inspired it was very bleak. Some of us may identify with that, in a way. Some of us may find ourselves crying out like the Psalmist that God doesn't seem to be working in our generation. Some of us may see very little evidence of His sovereignty and His benevolence in our lives, let alone in the world.

Why does God seem to hold back when His people suffer?

The Psalmist doesn't stay stuck in his lament, though. He lifts his eyes away from the detail of his own personal experience and examines the larger nature of God's work. The earth keeps turning. The oceans stay in their place. Day follows night. Spring follows winter.

All of it shows that God is still powerful, and God is still working with us. So, if you are struggling to see the work of God in your life, be encouraged by the dawning of a new season. As I write this, it is moving into autumn in South Africa, and it reminds me that God continues to bring new seasons. God continues to bring new life. God continues to bring new hope. God continues to sustain the world so that He can continue to redeem it.

Prayer:

Father God, I acknowledge that some days I struggle to see how you are working in the world. Give me eyes to see how you continue to show grace toward us, though. Let the simple things like the changing of the seasons speak afresh of your goodness toward us.

Psalm 75

Thankful Thinking

Reading:

Read the entire psalm, and then come back to read verse 1 again.

> *We give thanks to you, O God;*
> > *we give thanks, for your name is near.*
> *We recount your wondrous deeds.*
> > *Psalm 75:1*

Reflection:

I am the lifelong beneficiary of a very blessed upbringing. While I like to think that I grew up very simply, the truth is that I had a wonderfully privileged platform to work from. I never went hungry, I have a loving family, I never experienced intense sickness, and I had access to top-level primary, secondary, and tertiary education. It is good to reflect on those blessings, and that's really the point.

One of the curses of the human condition is that we are never really satisfied. We have a never-ending desire for more and a deluded notion that we will one day be satisfied with just a little more. We know all too well, though, that those who have the most seem to be least satisfied with their lot. With our eyes fixed always on the next acquisition, we can turn into a very sad people who seldom stop to consider what we already have.

Psalm 75 was written at a difficult time. Asaph, the author of this psalm, knew that God was still faithful to Israel, but the truth is that it was looking pretty bleak. Asaph also knew that they deserved nothing from God, and he was reflective on the very nature of God's supremacy and sovereignty. He knew that at any point, God could pull it all down; therefore, the fact that he was even breathing was evidence of God's grace toward him.

How thankful are you for what you have? How able are you to recognize God's gracious work in your life even in the midst of suffering and struggle?

I love Philippians 4. It asks us to be joyful, and then it tells us how.

> Do not be anxious about anything, but in everything by prayer and supplication with thanksgiving let your requests be made known to God. And the peace of God, which surpasses all understanding, will guard your hearts and your minds in Christ Jesus.
>
> Philippians 4:6–7

Continue to ask God for stuff, because He cares for you deeply and doesn't want you to be anxious. But do it with thanksgiving. Start with an audit of His goodness toward you.

That brings joy. That brings peace.

Prayer:

Father God, I come to you today not to ask you for anything, but to thank you for all you have already given me. You have been very kind to me, and I am thankful for what I have.

Psalm 76

Faithful Fear

Reading:

Read the entire psalm, and then read the following verses again.

> ⁶ *At your rebuke, O God of Jacob,*
>   *both rider and horse lay stunned.*
> ⁷ *But you, you are to be feared!*
>   *Who can stand before you*
>   *when once your anger is roused?*
>   *Psalm 76:6–7*

Reflection:

If God is like the God of the Bible, then He is to be feared. The Bible even says so repeatedly.

> The fear of the LORD is the beginning of wisdom,
> and knowledge of the Holy One is understanding.
>   Proverbs 9:10 (NIV)

How does that fit into the picture that we have been painting through the Psalms so far, of a loving God who does not hold our sin against us? Haven't we been exposed to a God who loves us and a God who stays with us in suffering and pain? Why should we fear that God? There is a tension here, isn't there? The Bible is full of tensions, and it makes no apologies for that. One of my good friends told me that the most important word in theology is *and*. I think I agree with him.

God is good AND God is sovereign.

God is loving AND God is just.

Christ does all the work of salvation AND we must work out our salvation with fear and trembling.

God knows the future AND we are responsible for our choices.

God is to be loved AND God is to be feared.

What we mustn't do is try to remove the tension in order to make God more understandable or even more palatable. He won't fit in a box we build for Him, and we shouldn't desire him to be able to. I worry that maybe some of us have removed the fear of the Lord from our understanding of who He is. He is absolutely holy and fundamentally opposed to sin and rebellion—so much so that He allowed His Son to be crucified in our place for our sins, so that His anger against our rebellion was absorbed.

If God is who He says He is in the Scriptures, then He should be feared, obeyed, loved, and worshipped, because He is all-powerful, entirely holy, absolutely good, eternally merciful, and unwaveringly faithful.

Fear Him. Love Him. Live for Him.

Prayer:

Heavenly Father, forgive me for when my view of you has been too small. Teach me more and more to fear you, love you, and live for you.

Psalm 77

Keep the Faith

Reading:

Read the entire psalm, and then read the following verses again.

> 7 *"Will the LORD spurn forever,*
> *and never again be favorable?*
> 8 *Has his steadfast love forever ceased?*
> *Are his promises at an end for all time?*
> 9 *Has God forgotten to be gracious?*
> *Has he in anger shut up his compassion?" Selah*
> 10 *Then I said, "I will appeal to this,*
> *to the years of the right hand of the Most High."*
> 11 *I will remember the deeds of the LORD;*
> *yes, I will remember your wonders of old.*
> 12 *I will ponder all your work,*
> *and meditate on your mighty deeds.*
> *Psalm 77:7–12*

Reflection:

I sound like a record stuck on repeat, but I love the honesty of the Psalms. They are good for the soul of a struggler like me. In Psalm 77, Asaph was really honest on three fronts. First, in the first few verses, he was honest about his level of distress. He honestly proclaimed that his soul refused to be comforted. That isn't something that you will hear from many pulpits, but it is in the Bible.

Second, in the middle of the psalm, Asaph explained his struggle to believe in the faithful nature of God. He asked questions that would get us kicked out of church today, like, "Has God forgotten to be gracious?"

Last, in the final section of the psalm, Asaph was honest about his desire for faith. He refused to give up in his quest for faith and faithfulness. He couldn't see the work of God in his current circumstances, so he went back to God's work in history, and he held on to that knowledge.

Asaph truly helps us in our journey of faith. Some of us need to be honest about how desperate we actually are. Behind our designer clothes and well-rehearsed smiles, many of us are coming undone. We think that the message of the gospel means that we have to be fine when in fact the message of the gospel only starts to grip us when we acknowledge we aren't fine.

Some of us need to ask some questions that could get us kicked out of church. Has God forgotten? A lot of us think it; not many of us ask it. Asaph did, and we can.

Some of us need to fight for faith by reading the Scriptures to remind ourselves of God's faithfulness to millions who have gone before us. If we can't clearly see His work in our lives, at least we can see His work in theirs, and that can build our faith.

Please be honest with where you really are, and please be relentless in your fight for the faith that will move you from there.

Prayer:

Father God, forgive me for the times when I have pretended to be doing better than I really am. Sometimes, I struggle to see how you are working in my life. Teach me to examine your work through the ages and to live full of faith that you are the same yesterday, today, and forever.

Psalm 78

God's Gracious Memory

Reading:

Take time to read the entire psalm. It is a long and tough read about God's judgment against a continuously rebellious people. Then, come back to read the following verses again.

> 35 *They remembered that God was their rock,*
>   *the Most High God their redeemer.*
> 36 *But they flattered him with their mouths;*
>   *they lied to him with their tongues.*
> 37 *Their heart was not steadfast toward him;*
>   *they were not faithful to his covenant.*
> 38 *Yet he, being compassionate,*
>   *atoned for their iniquity*
>   *and did not destroy them;*
>   *he restrained his anger often*
>   *and did not stir up all his wrath.*
> 39 *He remembered that they were but flesh,*
>   *a wind that passes and comes not again.*
>   Psalm 78:35–39

Reflection:

Psalm 78 is scary, and I think the main reason for that isn't the revelation that God judges wickedness—I am perfectly happy with the Creator of the universe calling out His creation on their rebellion—but rather that the faithlessness described in the psalm is a lot like the faithlessness I display every day. Even when the people repent, they flatter and lie and make a lot of promises they don't keep.

Praise God, then, that it says that God remembered that they were just flesh. God remembers our frailty and our weakness, and, according to the Psalmist, He atones for the iniquity of weak and fallen, fleshly creatures.

I am very thankful that God remembers how weak I am. How about you?

Prayer:

Father God, I am weak and fallen. Thank you that you remember my weakness, and that you pay for that fallen condition in the sacrifice of your Son. You have atoned for my iniquity through your compassion. I am very grateful.

Psalm 79

Why We Can't "Just Move On"

Reading:

Read the entire psalm, and then come back to read the following verse again.

> *Do not hold against us the sins of past generations;*
> *may your mercy come quickly to meet us,*
> *for we are in desperate need.*
> *Psalm 79:8 (NIV)*

Reflection:

I lived through the dying breaths of the wicked system of apartheid in South Africa. It was a tumultuous but mainly magical time, and the world looked on and marveled at the new, darling democracy of the South. It seemed miraculous that a nation previously so divided could emerge into a new people united under one flag. Over 20 years later, South Africans are still trying to figure out how to make that work. It has proved to be impossible without properly looking back and repenting of our past. We can't just move on, it seems, and that shouldn't surprise us when so much sin has been committed and so much injustice continues as a direct result of those systems.

Psalm 79 is a community lament. It is a song of sorrow and repentance after the Babylonians had left Jerusalem in ruins. Asaph doesn't think it is possible for Israel to just move on. He wanted them to sit in what they had done for a bit and to understand why they were where they were.

When I look at so much of the injustice that takes place in the world, much of it is a result of generations-old thinking and systems that perpetuate and exacerbate our wickedness. The Scriptures call us to repent, not just of where we are, but also of how we got to be where we are. We don't do that enough.

Verse 8 of Psalm 79 is my prayer as a white South African, but I think it fits almost anywhere in the world. Pray it with me.

Prayer:

Father God, do not hold against us the sins of our fathers. Give us the boldness and humility to be a generation that addresses those sins, and move us away from their ongoing impact.

Psalm 80

You Are a Fixer Upper

Reading:

Read the entire psalm, and then read the following verse again.

> *Restore us, O Lord God of hosts!*
> *Let your face shine, that we may be saved!*
> *Psalm 80:19*

Reflection:

I have a slightly strange interest in (read, "obsession with") vintage musical instruments. At one stage I owned three vintage guitars, even though I don't know how to play guitar. I just love the craftsmanship, the attention to detail, and the sheer beauty of something that can't quite be captured in any product made on a mass production line.

One day, a few years ago, I got a call from a friend of mine who is a dealer in vintage gear, and he insisted that I see him as soon as I could. He thought he had something I definitely wanted to see and probably wanted to own. He was right.

What he had was a 1954 Sonor Signature Maple drum kit. It was as rare as hens' teeth, but it was in really bad shape. It had been bought new in 1954 by a young man who married shortly after the purchase, only to discover that his new bride didn't share his passion for the drums. So, the kit had been dumped into poorly ventilated storage and had stayed there for over fifty years. The lugs were rusted, the shell covers were peeling, and the hardware was falling apart. When we pulled the original vellums off, though, we could see who she really was. The Canadian maple shells were perfect, and the hand-sanded bearing edges were as smooth as on the day that some German perfectionist had first sanded them down. In order for the kit to be playable, though, she needed restoration, and a lot of it. Through months of hard work, we got the kit restored to original condition, and the first time I took her out to a gig, I will never forget the way she sang. Her snare drum literally shouted out the glory and renown of God.

In Psalm 80, Asaph was crying out in desperation to God on behalf of the people of Israel. He was asking God to restore her to her former glory. This is the remarkable thing about the gospel, and indeed about the nature of our great God. Not only does He save us with His salvation, He also then restores us and makes us new again so that we can sing for His glory and renown.

Maybe you feel a bit like that old Sonor Signature? Through neglect, abuse, or even rebellion, you feel tainted, rusted, and dirty, and as a result you don't feel like you can sing a song of praise to God.

He is the great restorer. He is making you new. He won't stop until He is done. You will sing again.

Prayer:

Father God, thank you that you are the great restorer. Thank you that you don't just save us, but you also change us through the powerful message of your gospel. Keep doing your work in and on us. Restore us, God. Make us sing!

Psalm 81

Open Your Mouth

Reading:

Take time to read the entire psalm, and then read the following verse again.

> *I am the LORD your God,*
> *who brought you up out of the land of Egypt.*
> *Open your mouth wide, and I will fill it.*
> *Psalm 81:10*

Reflection:

Psalm 81 reads as a history of God interacting with His people Israel. Some parts of it are even written in the first person, with God Himself speaking to Israel about how He had experienced the relationship. An honest reading suggests that He sounds frustrated at the pig-headedness of His people.

One of the things that had frustrated God, according to Psalm 81, is the lack of trust that the people had shown Him in spite of His faithfulness through generations. In verse 10, He reminded them of the way that He rescued them from Egypt, and then asked them why they didn't trust Him more to provide abundantly for them.

The language that He used describes a baby bird opening its mouth in total desperation, but in total trust that its mother would feed it. That's how God wants His people to be. So that is exactly how I have been picturing myself in prayer today.

Totally desperate.
Totally dependent.
Totally sure.
Totally trusting.

God has proven Himself to be faithful through the ages. When will we learn to trust Him like this?

Prayer:

Father God, forgive me for being so quick to forget your faithfulness toward me, and equally quick to forget my total dependence upon you. Thank you for the way you feed, nourish, love, and protect me. Please don't stop.

Psalm 82

Pray for Politicians

Reading:

Read the entire psalm, and then read the following verses again.

> 2 *"How long will you judge unjustly*
>   *and show partiality to the wicked? Selah*
> 3 *Give justice to the weak and the fatherless;*
>   *maintain the right of the afflicted and the destitute.*
> 4 *Rescue the weak and the needy;*
>   *deliver them from the hand of the wicked."*
>   Psalm 82:2–4

Reflection:

It is impossible to escape politics. Some believers I know feel that faith and politics don't and cannot mix, but it is pretty clear that the Psalmists didn't believe that. Politics impact people—usually the most vulnerable of people—and God cares about those people.

As I write this, South Africa finds itself in the midst of a fascinating (and sometimes quite scary) political season, and the US is struggling in the aftermath of its most divisive presidential election ever. Politics is on the lips of pretty much everyone you run into. For some, there is renewed hope during political seasons—maybe a new person in office, or an old person in office with greater backing, will be able to bring about the change we have all been waiting for. For others, there is a growing sense of despondency that maybe nothing actually changes, and that we will see the same circus regardless of which clowns we elect.

Psalm 82 describes a day when God will call world leaders into His courtroom to give an account for the manner in which they have led. That brings me a mix of encouragement and terror. It means that morally bankrupt leaders won't get away with it forever, but it also means that it will be a terrifying day for many.

Eugene Peterson captures it well in The Message:

> [1] God calls the judges into his courtroom,
>   he puts all the judges in the dock.

> [2-4] "Enough! You've corrupted justice long enough,
>   you've let the wicked get away with murder.
> You're here to defend the defenseless,
>   to make sure that underdogs get a fair break;
> Your job is to stand up for the powerless,
>   and prosecute all those who exploit them."

> [5] Ignorant judges! Head-in-the-sand judges!
>   They haven't a clue to what's going on.
> And now everything's falling apart,
>   the world's coming unglued.

> [6-7] "I commissioned you judges, each one of you,
>   deputies of the High God,
> But you've betrayed your commission
>   and now you're stripped of your rank, busted."

⁸ O God, give them their just deserts!
You've got the whole world in your hands!
Psalm 82:1–8 (MSG)

Don't get despondent. Pray for your politicians. Be a good citizen. One day those in leadership over us will be judged by the greatest leader ever.

Prayer:

Father God, I pray for those in leadership over us. Convict them, empower them, use them. I also pray that I would do my part in defending the cause of the weak and the needy. Give me eyes to see the part I have to play.

Psalm 83

I Don't Know

Reading:

Read the entire psalm. It is a tough one to stomach. Then, come back to read the following verses again.

> [13] *O my God, make them like whirling dust,*
>   *like chaff before the wind.*
> [14] *As fire consumes the forest,*
>   *as the flame sets the mountains ablaze,*
> [15] *so may you pursue them with your tempest*
>   *and terrify them with your hurricane!*
> [16] *Fill their faces with shame,*
>   *that they may seek your name, O Lord.*
> [17] *Let them be put to shame and dismayed forever;*
>   *let them perish in disgrace,*
> [18] *that they may know that you alone,*
>   *whose name is the Lord,*
>   *are the Most High over all the earth.*
>   *Psalm 83:13–18*

Reflection:

There is a powerful phrase far over-used in government departments and far under-used by theologians.

"I don't know."

That would be my answer to you if you asked me how Psalm 83 fits into the rest of Scripture. I don't totally understand it. It is a very difficult passage, and it seems to fly in the face of a lot of the teachings we have in Scripture about how we should respond to our enemies.

I actually love it when Scripture does this, though. It builds my faith, instead of shrinking it. I think the notion of a God who could be fully described and understood is nonsensical. The Bible gives us everything we need for life and godliness, but it allows some mysteries to remain, and that's wonderful. It drives me in worship to Romans 11, that says:

> [33] Oh, the depth of the riches and wisdom and knowledge of God! How unsearchable are his judgments and how inscrutable his ways!
> [34] "For who has known the mind of the LORD,
> or who has been his counselor?"
> [35] "Or who has given a gift to him
> that he might be repaid?"
> [36] For from him and through him and to him are all things. To him be glory forever.
> Amen.
> Romans 11:33–36

I don't understand Psalm 83, and that's okay. In fact, it's a good thing. Celebrate some mystery every now and then.

Prayer:

Father God, I just acknowledge my station and position as a creature before you. I don't know what you know and don't see what you see. Help me steward my limitations through faith and trust in you.

Psalm 84

The Dog Ate My Homework

Reading:

Read the entire psalm, and then read the following verses again.

> ¹ *How lovely is your dwelling place,*
>   *O LORD of hosts!*
> ² *My soul longs, yes, faints*
>   *for the courts of the LORD;*
>   *my heart and flesh sing for joy*
>   *to the living God.*
>   *Psalm 84:1–2*

Reflection:

I like to claim I am something of a stoic individual. It suits my persona to think that I am moderate and temperate in all things. It also suits my particular preference of flavor for local church community. We are moderate people in life, and we are therefore moderate in our gatherings.

The problem is that it plainly isn't true.

I can't sit down when I watch international rugby (for my American friends, this is like football, but without pads, and against other countries). I run the danger of turning into a drooling, yelling, hissing imbecile when refereeing decisions don't go our way. I jump up and down at a U2 concert like an 8-year-old girl at a private Bieber show. I am still an excitable fellow. It is just to my shame that I seldom express that level of excitement over the notion that God is alive and available for me to engage with Him. Surely, that is something to get excited about, but tragically I seldom do.

In Psalm 84, the Sons of Korah are very excited about going to the temple. They are bordering on fainting they are so excited. The reason for this is that in their day, the temple held the presence of the living God, and the thought of a mere mortal being able to experience that presence in some way was enough to drive them into deep longing.

What about today? Today there isn't a temple in Jerusalem in which God dwells. The Scripture says that God's dwelling today is way more exciting than it was for the Sons of Korah.

> Don't you know that you yourselves are God's temple
> and that God's Spirit dwells in your midst?
> 1 Corinthians 3:16 (NIV)

> And in him you too are being built together to become
> a dwelling in which God lives by his Spirit.
> Ephesians 2:22 (NIV)

Today, God dwells in His people. That means that His divine presence is available to His children all the time. We should be very excited about that. Yet, we allow silly things like the busyness of life to dictate our time spent enjoying His presence. It has been said that the excuse of, "I don't have the time," is the adult equivalent of, "the dog ate my homework." It is just lame. How can we not have time to do the very thing that gives life meaning and purpose?

So, today, carve out some time to run to the courts of the Lord. Let your heart grow excited as you imagine what great mysteries He may share with you, and what great power He may bestow on you.

He is waiting.

Prayer:

Father God, give me a longing for you and for your presence. Forgive me for not having that longing and for not prioritizing time with you. I long for more of you.

Psalm 85

Believe Then Behave

Reading:

Read the entire psalm, and then read the following verses again.

> ¹ Lᴏʀᴅ, *you were favorable to your land;*
>   *you restored the fortunes of Jacob.*
> ² *You forgave the iniquity of your people;*
>   *you covered all their sin. Selah*
> ³ *You withdrew all your wrath;*
>   *you turned from your hot anger.*
>   Psalm 85:1–3

Reflection:

The Bible is filled with stories of people just as rebellious and foolish as we are. It's one of the reasons I find it so encouraging and joyful to read. It would seem that I am not alone in my own peculiar case of rebellion. I am acting out what my forefathers have done since Eve couldn't keep her hands off the fruit. I am still responsible for my rebellion, to be sure, but I am not the first to think of these ways to rebel.

But how do we change? How can we rebel less? Surely there is hope for a better kind of us? Didn't Jesus come to reinstate a new kind of man?

Again, the Bible is very helpful, as it outlines time and time again a process for change.

It goes: BELIEVE and then BEHAVE.

Unfortunately, we seem to have gotten the process reversed. I always seemed to think that if I BEHAVED then I would grow in my BELIEF. The problem with this was I didn't know how to behave, and I didn't really want to, either.

In Psalm 85, we have this process outlined for us once again. The Psalmist starts the psalm with a right BELIEF about God. God shows favor, and He forgives, and He covers sin, and He turns away from righteous anger (Psalm 85:1–3). What a wonderful God He is.

As a result of this BELIEF comes the hope for new BEHAVIOR.

> Let me hear what God the LORD will speak,
>> for he will speak peace to his people, to his saints;
>> but let them not turn back to folly.
>>> Psalm 85:8

If God is like He says He is, then we need to BEHAVE in a certain way, and we can. We can't just return to our folly once we know what He is like, can we?

If you are struggling for change, I would ask you what you BELIEVE about God. If you believe that He needs you to change your BEHAVIOR before He will love you, then I am afraid that your behavior will never change.

If you believe that He is gracious, merciful, compassionate, loving, and altogether righteous toward you in spite of your behavior, then you have the seed that can grow into some kind of life change.

BELIEVE, and then BEHAVE.

Prayer:

Father God, forgive me for the many ways I rebel. At the heart of all that rebellion is wrong belief about you—please forgive me for that. Return me to right belief about you and let that belief by the power of your Spirit begin to change me.

Psalm 86

What Is God Like?

Reading:

Read the entire psalm, and then read the following verse again.

> *For you, O LORD, are good and forgiving,*
> *abounding in steadfast love to all who call upon you.*
> *Psalm 86:5*

Reflection:

A.W. Tozer famously said, "What comes into our minds when we think about God is the most important thing about us."[16] In other words, the most important thing about you is what you think about when you think about God.

So, what do you think about when you think about Him?

At various stages in my life, I have encountered people who thought about God as:

> An angry and vengeful, troll-like figure out for their destruction. This is bad because it means that you don't

---

16. A. W. Tozer, *The Knowledge of the Holy* (New York: HarperCollins, 1961), 1.

want to be close to Him, and you certainly don't feel loved and forgiven by Him. So, you tend to just stay away from Him.

An old, grandpa-like being who is sweet as anything, but past his best. This is bad because it means that He isn't actually able to help, and it also means that His principles don't really fly in the new world. So, you are free to come up with a better way that suits your generation better.

A mystical, unknowable type of vapor just blowing around like the wind. This is bad because He seems to hide from you, and you can't take your problems to a vapor.

There is a repeat description of what God is like in Scripture, though. David quotes it in Psalm 86:5.

> For you, O LORD, are good and forgiving,
>   abounding in steadfast love to all who call upon you.

If that is what God is like, then He is worth knowing, loving, and worshipping. If you think about God like this, then you can't help but want to go running into His presence. So, what's stopping you today?

Prayer:

Father God, forgive me for believing things about you that aren't true. Give me faith to trust the revelation that Scripture gives us of who you are.

Psalm 87

Grace Green Card

Reading:

Read the entire psalm, and then read the following verses again.

> *⁴ Among those who know me I mention Rahab and Babylon;*
> *behold, Philistia and Tyre, with Cush—*
> *"This one was born there," they say.*
> *⁵ And of Zion it shall be said,*
> *"This one and that one were born in her";*
> *for the Most High himself will establish her.*
> Psalm 87:4–5

Reflection:

I am a South African citizen. I carry the green SA passport with me when I travel, which entitles me to certain privileges and also restricts me from others. It speaks of who I am in the eyes of the international community.

My son Daniel was born in the USA (I can't help but scream out some Springsteen as I type that). He has a blue American passport, which entitles him to certain other privileges I don't have but also places certain restrictions on him that don't bind me. He has freer access to most of the world than I do, but I reckon I have a better chance in large parts of the Middle East.

Psalm 87 speaks of the divine privileges bestowed upon those born in Zion, God's own city. It tells of the tremendous birth rights given to those from the city that God called His own. This was way better than carrying a US passport. This was the guarantee of the full rights of sons and daughters of the King. This was diplomatic immunity and trust fund cash all rolled into one. The psalm then goes on to say something remarkable, though, and something that must have annoyed anyone who had a Jerusalem passport. It says,

> Among those who know me I mention Rahab and Babylon;
>   behold, Philistia and Tyre, with Cush—
>   "This one was born there," they say.

These were cities that were seen as wicked and abhorrent, and God says that in His grace there would be a day when people from those cities would be given the full birth rights of those from Zion. God held a green card lottery through salvation, and as a result we are all recipients of new passports.

The point of all of this is simple. It doesn't really matter where you are coming from, what matters is where God says you are going. Your past restrictions, because of your sin, don't have to eliminate you from your inheritance as a son and your citizenship in the new Jerusalem.

Just think of it, in the great passport and customs line in the sky, all of us who are in Christ can expect the warm greeting, "This one was born in Zion. Welcome home."

Prayer:

Father God, your grace is just so marvelous. Thanks for making me, a foreigner and alien, into a citizen of your great Kingdom. Help me start to represent that Kingdom well.

Psalm 88

Divine Despair

Reading:

Read the entire psalm, and then read the following verses again.

> ¹³ But I, O LORD, cry to you;
>   in the morning my prayer comes before you.
> ¹⁴ O LORD, why do you cast my soul away?
>   Why do you hide your face from me?
> ¹⁵ Afflicted and close to death from my youth up,
>   I suffer your terrors; I am helpless.
> ¹⁶ Your wrath has swept over me;
>   your dreadful assaults destroy me.
> ¹⁷ They surround me like a flood all day long;
>   they close in on me together.
> ¹⁸ You have caused my beloved and my friend to shun me;
>   my companions have become darkness.
> Psalm 88:13–18

Reflection:

Hanging out with Christians can be annoying at times. I should know, I do it for a living. What is one of the most annoying things about us as a people is our need for everything to resolve with a nice, theologically-sound ending, even when we have conversations about things that cannot possibly resolve this side of eternity.

In our attempts to show ourselves as faithful, we have denied all the tension of the great mysteries in life. It's why Christian music and art often seem so one-dimensional—they lack tension, and try to get to the resolution point instead of dwelling a little bit in the unresolved.

There is lots of space for the unresolved in Scripture, though. It would seem there is even space for a little despair. I would imagine this is great news for those of you in despair who think you have to pretend in church. The writer of Psalm 88 didn't even need to pretend in order to get published in the Bible. You should read it. It doesn't resolve. It is uncomfortably despairing.

What is interesting about it, though, is that even though the writer is close to having given up on life, he hasn't given up on God. He doesn't have a fake victorious hope; rather, he just has a glimmer that God might be who He said He is. And that is all he has, but that is enough.

So here are three things that the Psalmist says to do if you are a Christian in despair:

1. Keep believing in the nature and character of God. Even though everything around him screamed that God had abandoned him, the Psalmist still says,

   > ¹ Lord, you are the God who saves me;
   >   Day and night I cry out to you.
   > ² May my prayer come before you;
   >   turn your ear to my cry. (NIV)

   He still acknowledged God's Lordship, and he still believed that God was good enough to hear him, even though he couldn't see any evidence of God's activity.

2. Keep crying out to Him. The Psalmist hadn't sulked and given up; rather, he kept crying out and kept pleading. He was persistent in his desire for relief from God.

3. Hope and trust for an answer. Even in his despair, the Psalmist still believed in his ultimate deliverance.

So, if you are in despair, you don't have to pretend, but you also don't have to give up. Keep believing, keep trusting, keep hoping.

Prayer:

Father God, please hear my prayer. Even when I am in the depths of despair, I pray that you continue to hear me and to sustain me. Turn your ear to me, oh Lord.

Psalm 89

Lifesong

Reading:

Read the entire psalm, and then read the following verses again.

> *I will sing of the steadfast love of the*
>   *LORD, forever;*
> *with my mouth I will make known*
>   *your faithfulness to all generations.*
> *Psalm 89:1*

Reflection:

I said in my devotion on Psalm 86 that the most important thing about us is what we think about when we think about God. I reckon that the second most important thing about us is what we think about when we think about ourselves in light of what we think about God.

If God is who He says He is, then what do we exist for? What is the purpose and the point of our time here on this planet? It's a question that vexes and troubles everyone. Well, it should anyway.

The first couple of verses of Psalm 89 neatly capture what I think we exist for. It's a pretty good purpose statement for my remaining days on this earth. My life exists as a song that is sung about God's great love. My words should speak of His faithfulness in a way that impacts my kids, and their kids, and their kids. My story should be one of God's unrelenting love toward an unyielding rebel, so that others may know that love is available for them, too.

This focuses me and helps me pay attention to the right things. I deeply desire to live for the fame and glory of the one true God, and to make His faithfulness known to the generations to come.

What are you living for?

Prayer:

Father God, I want my life to count in a way that impacts future generations. Make my life a song of praise about you that will impact those who come after me.

SELAH POINT 3

In Psalm 89 we spoke about legacy, and what we would want our lives to be remembered for. In this reflection point—before moving on to the next book in the Psalms—it might be a good idea to commit some of those thoughts to paper.

Spend some time in prayer asking God what your spiritual legacy should be.

Write down some of the things you want to live toward.

Spend more time in prayer asking the Holy Spirit to empower you to live that way.

BOOK FOUR
(90 – 106)

The delightful study of the Psalms has yielded me boundless profit and ever-growing pleasure; common gratitude constrains me to communicate to others a portion of the benefit, with the prayer that it may induce them to search further for themselves.

— *C. H. Spurgeon*

The most valuable thing the Psalms do for me is to express the same delight in God which made David dance.

— *C.S. Lewis*

Psalm 90

Don't Bank on a Long Retirement

Reading:

Read the entire psalm, and then read the following verse again.

> *The years of our life are seventy,*
> *or even by reason of strength eighty;*
> *yet their span is but toil and trouble;*
> *they are soon gone, and we fly away.*
> Psalm 90:10

Reflection:

We are all getting older. There is simply no denying it. The mirror doesn't lie, and neither does the scale. One of the hectic things about getting older, though, is that your parents get much older at the same time. I am very fortunate to have both my parents still alive, and both of my wife's parents are alive, too. My in-laws are in their seventies, and my parents aren't far behind. While this doesn't sound that old, it is according to Moses, who wrote Psalm 90. He reckons that seventy is a good innings, and that eighty is above and beyond. He says something very troubling about that, though: most people will live to seventy or eighty and have very little to show for it, except trouble and sorrow. He also says that it will pass by quickly, and before we know it, we will be gone.

He is right. So, here is my charge to you today.

Make today count, because there is no promise of tomorrow.

Do the important things today.

Say "I love you" to the people you love.

Encourage someone even if you think they don't need it.

Share the gospel urgently with somebody.

Give something away, something that costs you.

Trust God in a reckless way, as if He controls tomorrow.

Do it now, or it will quickly pass, and we will all fly away.

Prayer:

Father God, forgive me for the time that I waste. Bring me an urgency to my obedience and pursuit of you. My time here will be short, so help me to live for my time with you.

Psalm 91

God's Protective Embrace

Reading:

Read the entire psalm, and then read the following verse again.

> *He will cover you with his feathers,*
> *and under his wings you will find refuge;*
> *his faithfulness will be your shield and rampart.*
> *Psalm 91:4 (NIV)*

Reflection:

I like playing golf. I know it seems like a foolish pursuit for someone with an eternal perspective, but I just like the game. It reminds me how much I need Jesus, and it humbles me with each and every misdirected blow (there are usually many of those). I normally come home from golf knowing full well where I fit in the universe. It's near the bottom of the pecking order.

A few years ago, I was playing golf at one of my favorite courses. I smashed a drive on a par 5, but I smashed it into an area of the course where no human had ever set foot. It was a long way off course, but I was determined to find it. I was half expecting to find Dr. Livingstone hiding out in the area I had to trek through. I found my ball, but as I walked toward it, thinking of the incredible recovery shot I was going to make, I got viciously attacked. I thought the end had come. I couldn't tell what had happened at first, but after my initial panic settled, I realized that I was simply encountering something that many Johannesburg residents encounter every day. No, not a knife-wielding man, but a Blacksmith Lapwing bird dive-bombing me because I had unwittingly gotten too close to a nest. After several frantic swipes with a 7 iron, I managed to get myself out of the danger zone of this admittedly tiny but ferocious bird, and I was able to look back on my ruthless attacker. I saw it, standing in its nest, wings outstretched, covering its young.

My heart broke.

My mind went straight to Psalm 91.

This pose of a fearless and loving defender bird is how Moses described the posture of God over His children. It is said that Moses wrote this psalm as the Israelites entered the desert, and Moses knew there was trouble ahead for them. But, his picture of God was the picture of a bird protecting his young. Fearlessly, selflessly, sacrificially defending and protecting. What a picture.

I needed that picture again today. Maybe you did, too.

Prayer:

Father God, thank you that you stand in protection over me. Teach me to trust in your goodness. Cover me with your wings.

Psalm 92

Church Services Are Supposed to be Fun

Reading:

Take time to read the entire psalm, and then read the following verses again.

> ¹ It is good to give thanks to the LORD,
>   to sing praises to your name, O Most High;
> ² to declare your steadfast love in the morning,
>   and your faithfulness by night,
> ³ to the music of the lute and the harp,
>   to the melody of the lyre.
> ⁴ For you, O LORD, have made me glad by your work;
>   at the works of your hands I sing for joy.
>   Psalm 92:1–4

Reflection:

One of the truly cool things about being a follower of Christ is that we are not left to figure it out on our own. When we get new life in Christ, we also get a new family and a new community—that is, the church.

Just like every family, she has her issues, and this new family will not always be easy to get along with. But she is glorious.

One of the great joys, then, of being part of this new family is gathering together as a collective to corporately express praise, gratitude, and worship to our common God. These gatherings, which are undeniably encouraged for all believers in the Scripture, are the basis for what we now know as church services. They are designed to be inspiring and invigorating collective experiences of the divine, but somehow we seem to have made them into something much more mundane, boring, weird, and irrelevant than what they were supposed to be.

Psalm 92 lays out what it should be like when we get together to sing.

So, how about we approach Sundays with this mindset when we gather? It is good to praise the Lord. In order to get ourselves into that space, I have a few practical recommendations for us as we gather to sing together this weekend. Perhaps consider making this part of your routine.

1. Be early. There is nothing as distracting as being late and stressed. It will take you four songs to settle down, and by then some guy will be preaching, which will only serve to make you more stressed. Leave home early, and then take your time.

2. Be prepared. Read the first four verses of Psalm 92, as it will remind you of what we are actually doing together. We are such a distracted people, so it usually takes a while to focus. Try to focus beforehand, so that when the band strikes up, you are good to go.

3. Be proactive. I often hear of people critiquing the song order or arrangements, and saying that they couldn't get into it up until a particular moment. Don't wait for the moment, but determine that God is worthy of your whole-hearted praise, regardless of what the band might be playing. Just go for it, and hope the band catches up.

4. Be open. Maybe the style, volume, or song selection won't be exactly as you would have hoped, but do your best to remember that you are part of a collective and that it might well be best for the majority of the people around you. Instead of being a closed criticizer, be an open partaker. They tend to be the ones who get the joy.

I hope that helps you prepare for gathering as a people this weekend. I am so excited to be part of a collective worshipping together again this Sunday.

Prayer:

Father God, forgive me for the times when I have not been properly thoughtful and joyful about singing songs of praise and worship to you. Teach me to worship you in spirit and truth, and to do that in thousands of ways that aren't just singing. Teach me, too, the joy of what it means to sing of your faithfulness.

Psalm 93

Jesus vs. the Storm

Reading:

Read the entire psalm, and then read the following verses again.

> ³ *The floods have lifted up, O Lord,*
> *the floods have lifted up their voice;*
> *the floods lift up their roaring.*
> ⁴ *Mightier than the thunders of many waters,*
> *mightier than the waves of the sea,*
> *the Lord on high is mighty!*
> *Psalm 93:3–4*

Reflection:

Johannesburg is apparently the largest city in the world not built on a major waterway. It is one of the reasons I am really fond of the place and really grateful I was born and raised here. Large bodies of water freak me out, and I am grateful that God put some gold in the ground hundreds of kilometers away from the sea so that Jozi would be founded and I could grow up without the daily terror of death by shark, rip current, giant squid, vampire mermaid, irritated sperm whale, jellyfish infestation, 1, 230, 981, 723 blue bottle stings, or some other aquatic-related, terrifying death that will almost certainly befall you should you venture into the ocean.

The sea is terrifying.

It's so big and angry and hostile and relentless.

Think about it—it never stops pounding the beach, even when it is obvious that the rocks have become sand. It just keeps on coming. The Psalmist describes this terror and fury in Psalm 93, and he seems to agree with me that the sea is almost unnecessarily aggressive and scary. But then he says that God is mightier than the sea and the waves. That is a beautiful picture for me, because nothing seems stronger than the oceans. But God is. It makes me think of Jesus calming a great storm through the simple command of His voice. The disciples couldn't believe what they were seeing, and asked, "What kind of man is this? Even the winds and the waves obey him!" (Matt 8:27 NIV).

I am not sure what you might be facing at the moment, but maybe it feels as scary and un-relenting as the ocean. Just remember that Jesus has a habit of walking over stormy seas, and as the Psalmist says, our God is far mightier than the waves.

Trust Him in the storm.

Prayer:

Father God, teach me to take my eyes off of the storm and to keep them fixed on you. You are mighty, and you rule and reign over everything. Even the wind and waves obey your command. Teach me to trust you, Lord!

Psalm 94

Constant Consolation

Reading:

Take time to read the entire psalm, and then read the following verse again.

> *When the cares of my heart are many,*
> *your consolations cheer my soul.*
> *Psalm 94:19*

Reflection:

During one of my sermons recently, I made the observation that the life of a Christ-follower is tough by design. While it will and should have lots of joy, victory, and laughter, it isn't a guarantee of all daisies, rainbows, and unicorns, as some of the preachers on TV would have you believe.

The Scriptures never shy away from this fact, and never make light of human suffering, anxiety, discouragement, and doubt. In Psalm 94, the Psalmist is discouraged because he looks at the way the wicked prosper in the world while the innocent suffer. It brings him anxiety and stress, but he says that the Lord's consolation brings him joy.

So, here are a few simple truths from Scripture that I hope will bring you consolation amidst any anxiety you may struggle with.

1. You are fearfully and wonderfully made (Psalm 139). This means that your dignity, value, worth, and purpose are determined by your Creator and not by your boss, your spouse, your friends, your family, or what the magazines tell you.

2. Jesus is your friend if you follow Him (John 15:14). Of all the ways Jesus could have described His relationship with His followers, He called them friends. That never ceases to amaze me.

3. The temptation you currently face doesn't have to defeat or overwhelm you (1 Cor. 10:13). That means you aren't yet defeated and it is not inevitable that you will give in—so don't.

4. Jesus knows what it feels like to be tempted and will help you (Heb. 2:18). Again, this is an amazing truth. He knows what the suffering of temptation feels like, and He doesn't stand far off simply to condemn. He stands close by to assist.

5. Jesus is coming back to make all things right and reunite the living and the dead (1 Thess. 4:14). This is just flat-out good news. Hasten the day.

6. Your current circumstances don't confound God (Rom. 11:33–36). This means that while you may be perplexed, He isn't and never has been.

7. It is finished! The work of salvation is done, and we aren't under the condemnation of the law (Col. 2:13–15). This means there is great hope for all of us who believe.

Ponder on these things, be consoled, and then console others.

Prayer:

Father God, I acknowledge that most days the cares and concerns of my heart are many. Teach me to take great consolation in your promises and in your faithfulness.

Psalm 95

The Urgency of Obedience

Reading:

Read the entire psalm, and then read the following verses again.

> 6 *Oh come, let us worship and bow down;*
> *let us kneel before the LORD, our Maker!*
> 7 *For he is our God,*
> *and we are the people of his pasture,*
> *and the sheep of his hand.*
> 8 *Today, if you hear his voice,*
> *do not harden your hearts, as at Meribah,*
> *as on the day at Massah in the wilderness,*
> 9 *when your fathers put me to the test*
> *and put me to the proof, though they had seen my work.*
> *Psalm 95:6–9*

Reflection:

One of the objections people often make about the validity of the Bible is the claim that the Bible has inconsistencies and even contradictions. When one considers that the human instruments used to write the Scriptures are so varied, and so far from each other in terms of geography, life circumstances, and time, then I actually find the Scriptures to be remarkably consistent. It is amazing how much they reference each other, and how accurately they do it. It gives me confidence in its validity as a text.

The writer of the book of Hebrews (we are not entirely sure who it was) spends almost an entire chapter pondering Psalm 95 (read Hebrews 3 and 4). He uses it as a provocation, calling on his readers to use the opportunity that they have to obey God immediately, and in so doing to avoid being like their forefathers. These ancestors always assumed that they would obey one day in the future, but then ran out of future days to presume upon.

> Today, if you hear his voice,
> do not harden your hearts.

So, where is God speaking to you and asking for obedience?

Do you need to repent of something? Do it today.

Do you need to come clean about something you have done? Do it today.

Is God asking you for sacrificial generosity toward someone? Do it today.

Is God asking you to forgive? Do it today.

Is God asking you to follow Him into something, even though it looks risky? Do it today.

> Take care, brothers, lest there be in any of you an evil, unbelieving heart, leading you to fall away from the living God. But exhort one another every day, as long as it is called "today," that none of you may be hardened by the deceitfulness of sin.
>
> Hebrews 3:12–13

What are you waiting for?

Prayer:

Father God, thank you that today presents a fresh opportunity to follow you and to obey you. Grant me the courage to eliminate procrastination and to follow you fervently today.

Psalm 96

New Mercies and New Melodies

Reading:

Read the entire psalm, and then read the following verses again.

> *¹ Oh sing to the L*ORD *a new song;*
> *sing to the L*ORD*, all the earth!*
> *² Sing to the L*ORD*, bless his name;*
> *tell of his salvation from day to day*
> Psalm 96:1–2

Reflection:

Christians should be the most creative people on the planet. The Scriptures say that for us who are in Christ, there are new mercies from God every single morning. This means that every morning is a good morning, and every day is filled with reasons to find creative ways to tell the world the good news of His salvation.

The Psalmist who wrote Psalm 96 was determined. We need a new song! We have experienced new mercies! Let us not simply copy the songs and stories of old, because God has done something in our day.

So come on, you creative types. Let's stop being followers (and slow followers, at that) of culture, and let us unleash a multitude of new songs to the Lord. Write new songs, paint new pictures, craft new stories, because we have endless new mercies.

Your story of God's faithfulness toward you matters. Tell your story using what God has given you.

Prayer:

Father God, thank you for your abundant mercies. Teach me to tell others of those stories.

Psalm 97

All You Need Is Love...and Hate

Reading:

Read the entire psalm, and then read the following verses again.

> ¹⁰ *O you who love the* LORD, *hate evil!*
>   *He preserves the lives of his saints;*
>   *he delivers them from the hand of the wicked.*
> ¹¹ *Light is sown for the righteous,*
>   *and joy for the upright in heart.*
> ¹² *Rejoice in the* LORD, *O you righteous,*
>   *and give thanks to his holy name!*
>   *Psalm 97:10–12*

Reflection:

Psalm 97 has rattled my cage. I love it when the Bible does that. It gets under your skin, and into your business. It irritates and provokes by pushing and prodding on areas where you know you need some change. It does that to me pretty much every day.

Verse 10 has really convicted me. It says that those who love God should hate evil. Now, I know we don't want to come across as fundamentalist jerks or the caricatured Christian hater guys who throw stones continually at everyone around them,. I know I don't want to be that guy, but in my quest to not be that guy, I think I run the danger of being someone who misses the fact that part of my love for God is supposed to be a hatred of evil and wickedness. Maybe in our quest to understand and connect with culture, we have forgotten to hate the things God hates?

The real issue, though, starts with us and not with culture. Can we truly say we are people who hate our own sin and rebellion? Do we hate it enough to fight it, and do we hate it enough to flee from it when necessary?

I am praying for a fragile conscience and the discernment to hate the things God hates. I am starting with a long, hard look at the things in my own life.

Prayer:

Father God, teach me to hate what you hate. Give me eyes to see and a fragile conscience to discern and respond. Change my heart, oh God.

Psalm 98

More Is Less

Reading:

Read the entire psalm, and then come back to read the following verses again.

> ^{1} *Oh sing to the L*ORD *a new song,*
>   *for he has done marvelous things!*
> *His right hand and his holy arm*
>   *have worked salvation for him.*
> ^{2} *The L*ORD *has made known his salvation;*
>   *he has revealed his righteousness in the sight of the nations.*
> ^{3} *He has remembered his steadfast love and faithfulness*
>   *to the house of Israel.*
> *All the ends of the earth have seen*
>   *the salvation of our God.*
>   *Psalm 98:1–3*

Reflection:

It seems to me that we may well be one of the least satisfied generations of all time, which is very weird because we probably have more available to us than any of our predecessors. Yet, our "more" doesn't ever cross the threshold of "enough." It can't, because we have designed entire economic systems off the fact that we need to make sure people believe they constantly need more. We build industries to make stuff, then create other industries to convince people that they need the stuff. Why? Because the other stuff they once needed, well, they of course don't need that anymore. Finally, we make other industries that loan us money, because we simply can't take the time to save the money we would need to buy the stuff.

I know it sounds like a cynical assessment, but it is exactly how society is designed. We are programmed for dissatisfaction. This permanent quest for more has impacted the church as well, as Christians now want to know what more God can do for them. Churches that promise a God who gives us more can't keep up with the demand that people have to hear that message, and so they themselves end up replicating culture in a "must get more" methodology of church. They want more people giving in their church, and more people want more promises of prosperity. So, they scratch each other's backs.

What happens, though, when God doesn't give us what we think we are entitled to? What do we do when suffering, poverty, famine, and confusion come along? What happens to our faith when God doesn't seem interested in playing the more game with me?

We sulk. I see it all the time. We doubt His goodness and question His control, and then we withhold worship because we don't feel like we have anything to give Him praise for.

Psalm 98 is a song about celebrating God's goodness. It is really upbeat, so it might be a psalm that is difficult for someone who feels like they deserve more from God than they are getting. The thing is, the basis for God's goodness in the psalm is His salvation. It has nothing to do with what He gives or how He might bless materially or circumstantially; rather, it just celebrates that God offers the great news of new life to sinners and rebels, and this is reason enough for the Psalmist to sing.

Ephesians 1:3 says, "Blessed be the God and Father of our Lord Jesus Christ, who has blessed us in Christ with every spiritual blessing in the heavenly places." What Paul is saying is that anyone who knows Jesus, and what He has already done for them, is abundantly blessed. There is nothing better or more meaningful that God could possibly give them. Anything else is a trinket.

You don't need more than what you already have in Jesus!

So, are you looking for a reason for praise and thanks? If you know Jesus and His salvation, you have every reason in the world to praise, regardless of your circumstances. Your world could be going down the drain, but you have the news that God stooped down to redeem you. Nothing tops that.

Prayer:

Father God, teach me what it means to be satisfied in you, regardless of what faces me. Show me the glory and the wonder of the gift of salvation, and keep my heart from pursuing anything less.

Psalm 99

Does God Screen Our Calls?

Reading:

Read the entire psalm, and then read the following verse again.

> *O LORD our God, you answered them;*
> *you were a forgiving God to them.*
> *Psalm 99:8*

Reflection:

I screen my calls. I never used to, as it was quite exciting to get calls from anyone, but now I kind of have to; otherwise, I would be on the phone all day. If it's a private number, I don't answer, since I already have a cell phone contract and am not interested in purchasing another one from the cold caller. If it's one of my friends and I am busy with something, I will often let it go to voicemail and chat with them at a better time. I have good friends who give me grace in this area. If it's my wife, I will answer. It's a rude system, but it helps me function better.

What about God? Does He screen our calls? Do we have to leave a message if we call at an inconvenient time, or if we have been really bad and He is angry with us? Well, no, Scripture says that we can call on Him anytime, and He will answer us. Psalm 99 speaks of a God who answers, and it is an astonishing concept if you think about it. It also speaks of priests, though, who act as intermediaries on behalf of people. Do we need a priest in order to get in touch with God?

Yes, we do, but we have one who gets us right in there all the time. Hebrews 4:14–16 (NIV) says,

> Therefore, since we have a great high priest who has ascended into heaven, Jesus the Son of God, let us hold firmly to the faith we profess. For we do not have a high priest who is unable to empathize with our weaknesses, but we have one who has been tempted in every way, just as we are—yet he did not sin. Let us then approach God's throne of grace with confidence, so that we may receive mercy and find grace to help us in our time of need.

It's astounding, if you think about it. We get to approach the God of the universe with confidence because of the work of His Son on our behalf. When we approach God to tell Him that something is tough, Jesus is there on our behalf, saying, "I know, I know how that feels."

So, dear Christian, please pray. Pray all the time. It is absolute foolishness to not pray. You have the opportunity to have unlimited access to the throne room of the Most High. He doesn't screen, He is never unavailable, and He knows what you are going through.

Call.

Prayer:

Father God, forgive us for the fact that we fail to make the most of the open access we have to you through the work of your wonderful Son. I echo the plea of his disciples: Lord, teach us how to pray! Give us the confidence, humility, boldness, dependence, trust, and worship that we need.

Psalm 100

Shouting Sheep

Reading:

Read the entire psalm, and then read the following verses again.

> ^{1} *Shout for joy to the LORD, all the earth.*
> ^{2} *Worship the LORD with gladness;*
>   *come before him with joyful songs.*
> ^{3} *Know that the LORD is God.*
>   *It is he who made us, and we are his;*
>   *we are his people, the sheep of his pasture.*
>   *Psalm 100:1–3 (NIV)*

Reflection:

The last few weeks have been quite tough for me. My life is still good, and we still have much to be thankful for, but it has been a stressful time during which we have had to deal with death, loss, sickness, sin, rebellion, conflict, and pressure.

With that in mind, then, the first couple of verses in Psalm 100 irritated me this morning and drew out the rebel in me.

Shout for joy? I don't want to.

Worship with gladness? I don't feel glad.

But praise God for verse 3 that serves as a real tonic for my soul today, and makes verses 1 and 2 seem attainable again. Verse 3 reminds me that God made me and everyone else, and He gets to do whatever He wants with His creations. This sounds like a really scary proposition, because if God is cruel, then the fact that we are in His hands doesn't serve as good news, but rather as news of imminent destruction. But verse 3 goes on to describe God as a shepherd and us as His sheep. Shepherds by nature take care of their sheep, and so I can be confident that God takes care of me.

A good shepherd knows his sheep, so I know that God knows the details of my life, and that He cares for me in the mess, futility, and frustration of daily living.

A good shepherd feeds his sheep, so I know that God continues to bring truth to my situations so that I may know Him better and trust Him fully. Just this morning, the Spirit of God ministered to me deeply from the truth of the Scriptures, and as a result, my starving soul was fed.

A good shepherd leads his sheep, so I know God will lead and guide me through difficult decisions and tricky situations if I only ask Him.

A good shepherd protects his sheep, so I know that even though I am in over my head, I have nothing to fear. Not even death is a fearful thing for those under the care of the Good Shepherd.

When I remember all of that, then I want to shout for joy, and worship with gladness.

The Lord is my shepherd; I shall not be in want.

Prayer:

Father God, please remind me that I am yours, and that I can trust you with my life and with the lives of others around me. Let that knowledge lead to praise, God. I believe, but help my unbelief.

Psalm 101

Got Any Change?

Reading:

Read the entire psalm, and then read the following verses again.

> ¹ *I will sing of steadfast love and justice;*
>   *to you, O LORD, I will make music.*
> ² *I will ponder the way that is blameless.*
>   *Oh when will you come to me?*
> *I will walk with integrity of heart*
>   *within my house;*
> ³ *I will not set before my eyes*
>   *anything that is worthless.*
> *I hate the work of those who fall away;*
>   *it shall not cling to me.*
>   *Psalm 101:1–3*

Reflection:

"People don't change. He will never change."

I recently heard these words come out of the mouth of a betrayed wife, as she was walking away from a marriage that she had discovered to be a sham, as story after story of her husband's infidelity had come to light. He was broken and repentant and desired to fix the mess he had made, but her mind was made up—not based only on the wounding that she had received from her husband's rebellion and sin, but based on a worldview developed by watching people her entire life. In her experience, people didn't have the ability to change themselves into something different.

I knew how she felt, as not long before I had held the same worldview. It was a view established not so much on how people had failed me, but on how little I had managed to change myself through the years. But then something happened—I did change, and I saw people around me change, people for whom I had no hope left.

How?

Was it a secret formula, or a new book? Did a subscription to a magazine finally contain the right concoction to persuade us to change? Not in my case. What happened with me that began my process was that I got a clearer, truer picture of who God was. When I understood who He was, change was consequential, but when I focused on changing to get closer to God, I never succeeded.

Psalm 101 shows this to us as a pattern. The writer starts out by speaking about the nature of God, and then goes on to speak of a new kind of life that is lived as a result of an understanding of that nature. When we know, and I mean really know, that God is loving toward us, and absolutely just at the same time, then our lives quite simply have to look different from when we didn't have that knowledge.

Right living is a consequence of right belief and thought.

So, if you really want to change, spend less time thinking about change, and more time thinking about God. When you get the glory of who He is and who you are because of Him, you won't be able to prevent change.

Prayer:

Father God, teach me to think about your love, your justice, and your blamelessness, and allow that understanding of who you are to create change in me.

Psalm 102

The Futility of the Temporary

Reading:

Prayerfully read through the psalm in its entirety and then review the verses below again.

> ¹ Hear my prayer, O LORD;
>> let my cry come to you!
> ² Do not hide your face from me
>> in the day of my distress!
>
> Incline your ear to me;
>> answer me speedily in the day when I call!
> ³ For my days pass away like smoke,
>> and my bones burn like a furnace.
>> Psalm 102:1–3

Reflection:

Being a pastor places one in some fairly peculiar situations. You get special closeness with and access to people in moments when they keep others at a distance. You get to speak to brides before they are seen by all of their guests. You get to talk to grooms before they watch their bride walk down the aisle. You get called to hospitals in the early hours of the morning, and you get allowed into ICU rooms otherwise reserved for immediate families. You get to hold hands with people as doctors bring bad news, and you are asked to say words of comfort as coffins of loved ones are lowered into deep and permanent holes.

It is a crazy job, and a very special privilege. You get special insight into the seeming futility of the temporary. You know the fragility of human life more than most, and if you pay attention, you get a front row seat in the most profound lecture hall of human wisdom in the world. Recently, I have again been invited into some of these sacred spaces. I have watched people die. I am watching days vanish like smoke. Everything seems temporary, each moment seems precious, and the desperation to hang on to every second of this temporal experience hangs heavy in every cubic centimeter of the ICU air.

Seeing such things can lead one to a sense of futility about everything. Is this it? Is there anything that isn't temporary? The Psalmist thinks so.

> ²⁵ Of old you laid the foundation of the earth,
>   and the heavens are the work of your hands.
> ²⁶ They will perish, but you will remain;
>   they will all wear out like a garment.
> ²⁷ You will change them like a robe, and they will pass away,
>   but you are the same, and your years have no end.
> ²⁸ The children of your servants shall dwell secure;
>   their offspring shall be established before you.
>   Psalm 102:25–28

If the Bible is true (and it is), God isn't fighting for survival. He has existed forever, and He will continue to exist forever. If that is true, there is hope beyond the futility of the temporary. The Psalmist concludes that even though our physical bodies may disappear like smoke, there is something about us that lives in God's presence forever.

As a result, the temporary isn't futile. Fight for its meaning, value, and purpose. If there is eternal existence, then today matters, and it matters forever. Live like it does.

Prayer:

Father God, you are from everlasting to everlasting. I am not. Teach me to rely on you in my short few days here.

Psalm 103

God Knows I'm Human

Reading:

Read the entire psalm slowly. Then come back to read the following verses again.

> [8] *The LORD is merciful and gracious,*
>   *slow to anger and abounding in steadfast love.*
> [9] *He will not always chide,*
>   *nor will he keep his anger forever.*
> [10] *He does not deal with us according to our sins,*
>   *nor repay us according to our iniquities.*
> [11] *For as high as the heavens are above the earth,*
>   *so great is his steadfast love toward those who fear him;*
> [12] *as far as the east is from the west,*
>   *so far does he remove our transgressions from us.*
> [13] *As a father shows compassion to his children,*
>   *so the LORD shows compassion to those who fear him.*
> [14] *For he knows our frame;*
>   *he remembers that we are dust.*
> [15] *As for man, his days are like grass;*
>   *he flourishes like a flower of the field;*

> _¹⁶ for the wind passes over it, and it is gone,_
>   _and its place knows it no more._
> _¹⁷ But the steadfast love of the_ LORD _is from everlasting_
>   _to everlasting on those who fear him,_
>   _and his righteousness to children's children,_
> _¹⁸ to those who keep his covenant_
>   _and remember to do his commandments._
>   _Psalm 103:8–18_

Reflection:

I am only human.

It's an excuse we use for a variety of failings, and it sounds like a cop-out, to be honest. But, it is actually entirely biblical. Psalm 103 tells us that God looks down on us and knows we are human and prone to failure and, as a result, He meets us with a measure of love and grace we can't even begin to fathom. He doesn't give us what we deserve, and He isn't distant from us because of our repeated failures.

I love what David says in verse 12. Give it a read, and think about it. He removes my sins from me, and He takes them as far from me as the east is from the west. How far is that? Well, by my calculations, that is incalculable. Spurgeon spoke of this verse in this way:

> O glorious verse, no word even upon the inspired page can excel it! Sin is removed from us by a miracle of love! What a load to move, and yet is it removed so far that the distance is incalculable. Fly as far as the wing of imagination can bear you, and if you journey through space eastward, you are further from the west at every beat of your wing. If sin be removed so far, then we may be sure that the scent, the trace, the very memory of it must be entirely gone. If this be the distance of its removal, there is no shade of fear of its

ever being brought back again; even Satan himself could not achieve such a task. Our sins are gone, Jesus has borne them away.[17]

So, next time you fail, which won't be long from now, instead of thinking of the guilt and shame you need to place upon yourself in order to prove your contrition, think about how far the east is from the west, and celebrate the fact that God knows you are human. He loves you, forgives you, and restores you.

Prayer:

Father God, thank you for your mercy. Thank you for your love. I am only human, and you know that, and I am so thankful for that.

---

17. Spurgeon, *The Treasury of David, Volume 1*, 34.

Psalm 104

The Glory of Your Job

Reading:

Read the entire psalm, and then read the following verses again.

> ²¹ *The young lions roar for their prey,*
>   *seeking their food from God.*
> ²² *When the sun rises, they steal away*
>   *and lie down in their dens.*
> ²³ *Man goes out to his work*
>   *and to his labor until the evening.*
>   *Psalm 104:21–23*

Reflection:

Psalm 104 is a song of praise outlining the mercy and power of God as evidenced in the splendor of creation. It speaks of seas, rivers, grass, cattle, trees, birds, mountains, and moons as examples of the goodness and greatness of God. It speaks of changes in seasons as reminders of God's mercy, and then in verse 21, it speaks of something I can identify with: the worshipful roar of a lion. When you hear the deep roar of a lion at night in the African bush, you cannot help but believe, pray, and worship.

But then, verse 23 happens. The Psalmist speaks about getting up in the morning and going to work until it is dark, and the psalm hasn't suddenly shifted to speak of the curse of sin. It is still in the context of God's goodness and mercy. According to Scripture, my job, and your job, are evidences of God's grace, equal to the haunting roar of a lion on the African plains. It, too, should drive us to belief, prayer, and worship. It should remind us, at the very least, of our need for Him.

So, as you go out to work today, thank God, and work well. As you do that, you let out a roar of praise to your Maker that can be heard for miles.

Prayer:

Father God, thank you for bringing meaning to our work. Help us work in a way that brings glory and honor to your name. Forgive me for the way I often resent my job and fail to represent you well while I am working. Teach me to roar your praise while I work.

Psalm 105

Good Enough to Share

Reading:

Read the entire psalm, and then read the following verses again.

> *¹ Oh give thanks to the LORD; call upon his name;*
> *make known his deeds among the peoples!*
> *² Sing to him, sing praises to him;*
> *tell of all his wondrous works!*
> *Psalm 105:1–2*

Reflection:

I think the world would be a far better place if more followers of Christ found their voices and spoke to others of the goodness of God in their lives. It seems to me that the only "Christians" who are speaking loudly are the ones who should really be quiet, and in an effort to not be lumped with that category of religious nuts, everyone else has adopted a "personal relationship with Jesus that doesn't need to be shared with others." The only problem with that view of a relationship with God is the Bible. It speaks repeatedly of how the people of God are supposed to speak boldly of the goodness of God, and Psalm 105 gives us another example of that.

If God is good, then we need to let the nations know.

If God is wonderful, then we should be telling people about Him.

In an era where we are more than willing to share just about anything about ourselves to an online audience of billions, will we be people who at least share the most important thing in the universe with our neighbors, our families, and our co-workers?

How about we make it a daily prayer request that God would grant us opportunity to testify of His goodness? I think we will be amazed at how we would choose to answer that prayer.

Make known His deeds among the peoples.

Prayer:

Father God, forgive me for remaining silent when you have been so good to me and when I have great opportunity to share that. Embolden me to be your witness, and give me opportunity to speak of your goodness to others.

Psalm 106

God Saves for God's Sake

Reading:

Read the entire psalm, and then read the following verses again.

> ⁶ *Both we and our fathers have sinned;*
> *we have committed iniquity; we have done wickedness.*
> ⁷ *Our fathers, when they were in Egypt,*
> *did not consider your wondrous works;*
> *they did not remember the abundance of your steadfast love,*
> *but rebelled by the sea, at the Red Sea.*
> ⁸ *Yet he saved them for his name's sake,*
> *that he might make known his mighty power.*
> *Psalm 106:6–8*

Reflection:

Recently, in some of my sermons, I have been outlining where we as humans fit in the story of all things. I will give you a clue: it's not in the middle. We all matter, but nowhere near as much as we tend to think we do in the grand narrative of redemption. We have a desperate need to play the starring role and to be the center of everything. We deeply desire to be the point and the purpose of our own lives.

Christians have extended this desperate need for focus and meaning to salvation. God saves us for us, right? Well, unfortunately, according to Scripture, no.

Time and time again, Scripture reminds us that the center of the universe is God and not us. He is the hero of the story, who lovingly and graciously allows us to participate with Him in the telling of the great story of His salvation and redemption. And so, Psalm 106 reminds us again that even the salvation of God isn't about us. He saves us for Himself, and for the sake of His great name (v. 8).

This is uncomfortable, but it is really good news. It means that the pressure isn't on us. The psalm reminds us that it wasn't based on the loveliness of the Israelites that God acted (v. 7). He acted for the sake of His own name. This means that God's furious pursuit of His own glory is actually the most joyful doctrine in the world.

It isn't about me!

Now that's brilliant news.

God loves you way too much to let it be about you. He knows you couldn't stand that kind of pressure.

Prayer:

Father God, forgive me for the many ways I tend to make things about me. Help me live in the freedom of knowing I exist and have been redeemed for your glory. Teach me to trust you in that.

SELAH POINT 4

You are now more than two-thirds of the way through your study of the Psalms. I hope and pray that God has been speaking to you and that you have grown in your love for Him as you have gone along.

At this point of pause and reflection, it might be a good idea to give some of what you have learned some legs. Take a pause today and ask God in prayer what He would have you do as a result of what you have learned. What new behaviors do you need to start? What old behaviors do you need to stop? Ask the Spirit to guide you in knowing and to strengthen you in doing.

BOOK FIVE
(107–150)

The Psalms are a reality check to keep prayer from becoming sentimental, superficial, or detached from the real world.

— *Richard H Schmidt*

A psalm implies serenity of Soul; it is the author of peace, which calms bewildering and seething thoughts. For, it softens the wrath of the soul, and what is unbridled it chastens. A psalm forms friendships, unites those separated, conciliates those at enmity. Who, indeed, can still consider as an enemy him with whom he has uttered the same prayer to God? So that psalmody, bringing about choral singing, a bond, as it were, toward unity, and joining people into a harmonious union of one choir, produces also the greatest of blessings, love.

— *St. Basil the Great*

Psalm 107

Satisfaction Guaranteed

Reading:

Read the entire psalm, and then read the following verses again.

> ¹ *Oh give thanks to the* LORD, *for he is good,*
>   *for his steadfast love endures forever!*
> ² *Let the redeemed of the* LORD *say so,*
>   *whom he has redeemed from trouble*
> ³ *and gathered in from the lands,*
>   *from the east and from the west,*
>   *from the north and from the south.*
>   Psalm 107:1–3

Reflection:

John Piper said it best when he said, "God is most glorified in us when we are most satisfied in Him."[18] Thankful people are joyful people, and joyful people bring glory to God in a world where very few people can display the luminescent quality of joyful satisfaction.

---

18. John Piper, "God Is Most Glorified in Us When We Are Most Satisfied in Him," http://www.desiringgod.org/messages/god-is-most-glorified-in-us-when-we-are-most-satisfied-in-him.

Psalm 107 is an anthem of thanksgiving and satisfaction in God. It is a recollection of God's goodness in the lives of His people. We can struggle to identify with it, though, because we continually view the world through the lens of what we don't have, rather than looking at what we do have. We continue to judge the goodness of God based on all the things we perceive He hasn't done for us, rather than looking at all the things He has done.

Let us make every effort to look at our lives through the lenses of God's goodness and grace, and as we do that we will realize that there are signs all over the place of His mercy and love. That knowledge brings us joy, and that brings us satisfaction, and that brings us faith, and that brings Him glory.

Be thankful, for He is good.

Prayer:

Father God, you have been so good to me. Give me eyes to see how kind and gracious you have been. Teach me, Lord, what it means to be satisfied fully in you!

Psalm 108

The Center of a Spinning Wheel

Reading:

Read the entire psalm, and then read the following verses again.

> ^{1} *My heart is steadfast, O God!*
> *I will sing and make melody with all my being!*
> ^{2} *Awake, O harp and lyre!*
> *I will awake the dawn!*
> ^{3} *I will give thanks to you, O LORD, among the peoples;*
> *I will sing praises to you among the nations.*
> ^{4} *For your steadfast love is great above the heavens;*
> *your faithfulness reaches to the clouds.*
> ^{5} *Be exalted, O God, above the heavens!*
> *Let your glory be over all the earth!*
> *Psalm 108:1–5*

Reflection:

I know I am at risk of dulling my affections for Christ when I allow my emotions to take over my life for too long. Emotions are important, and we have seen that in the Psalms, but they are cruel masters and can cloud out reality quite quickly.

In Psalm 108, David—who was not a bastion of emotional stability—spoke about having a steadfast heart. Other translations have said that his heart was "fixed." In other words, it remained unmoved while all else moved around it. Circumstances could change, but his heart remained fixed on the goodness, faithfulness, and love of God. G. S. Bowes described it like this:

> The wheels of a chariot revolve, but the axletree turns not; the sails of a mill move with the wind, but the mill itself moves not; the earth is carried round its orbit, but its centre is fixed. So should a Christian be able, amidst changing scenes and changing fortunes, to say, "O God, my heart is fixed, my heart is fixed."[19]

There are certain things that fix my heart and center me on God's goodness. Reading my Bible does it. Prayer does it. Christian community does it. Long chats about life with my wife get it done too. My job is to make sure I am doing all I can to make my heart steadfast—then, when the storms come, I won't be blown around as a victim of my own emotions, but I will be able to stand firm in the knowledge of the goodness of God.

What about you? How steadfast is your heart? What can you do to ground and anchor it in God today?

Prayer:

Make my heart steadfast, God, so that I might be someone who keeps my hope in you regardless of what is going on around me.

---

19. G. S. Bowes in Spurgeon, *The Treasury of David, Volume 1*, 34.

Psalm 109

Praying Instead of Posturing

Reading:

Read the entire psalm. Warning: it is a tricky one. Then, come back to read the following verse again.

> *In return for my love they accuse me,*
> *but I give myself to prayer.*
> *Psalm 109:4*

Reflection:

Nothing stings quite so much in this life as discovering that friends have laid false accusations against you. People you know and love, and whom you thought loved you, have been saying unfair and untrue things about you, all the while keeping up the facade of friendship. It stings when that happens. David knew the scenario well, and in Psalm 109 he wrote about the depths of the agony he felt. It is a disturbing psalm in many ways, if you read the whole thing, as David prays for bad things to happen to the person who falsely accuses him. It doesn't seem to compute with the grace that Christ bestows on us, and maybe that's the point. Maybe it is meant to serve as a juxtaposition between how Christ treats His enemies and how we want to treat ours.

But David does say something amazing in verse 4 that has helped me recently. He says that the best response to an attack on one's identity is to pray. That is a brilliant piece of advice. It is a great reminder that we live for an audience of one and that what God thinks of us is much more important than what anyone else thinks. We are so desperate to be loved that we will automatically move to publicly defend ourselves from any type of potential rejection; but by going straight to prayer first, we declare that our identity is rooted and established in God, and that He gets to make the calls on who we are.

Just the other day, I had a situation where I felt that I should publicly defend my reputation. At the root of it was pride, though, so I went to the most humbling place, which is on my knees before the Almighty. When I emerged, it really didn't matter what anyone else thought or said, because I knew how much I was loved by the only One that matters.

Next time your identity and reputation are on the line, be a man or woman of prayer. It is counterintuitive, but it brings joy and freedom.

Prayer:

Father God, teach me to be someone so confident in you that I don't place my identity in the treatment I receive from other people. Forgive me for the ways I place more value on the approval of man than I do on your approval of who I am. Help me, Lord.

Psalm 110

A King Who Is a Priest, and a Priest Who Is a King

Reading:

Read the entire psalm, and then read the following verse again.

> *The LORD has sworn*
> > *and will not change his mind,*
> *"You are a priest forever*
> > *after the order of Melchizedek."*
> > > *Psalm 110:4*

Reflection:

The more I study Jesus and His claims, the more humbled, submissive, worshipful, and astonished I become. Jesus is astounding. He can be difficult to read about in many ways because He just refuses to fit into any box we try to put Him into. I am fairly persuaded that most modern churches wouldn't have the faintest idea what to do with Him if He arrived at a service one Sunday. He is just so massive, and so all-encompassing, that He is actually very difficult to understand. It's by design. We shouldn't be able to fully explain God.

Psalm 110 speaks about Him long before He enters the world as a man. It starts off by saying that He will be a combination of the Son of David and the Lord of David. He will be from David's birth-line, but He actually made the world that David was born into. It's wild if you think about it.

But then it goes on to say that He will not only be a man who is God, but that He will be God, who is a man.

He will be our high priest forever.

The high priest was man's representative before a holy God. He offered sacrifices on man's behalf and represented the prayers and pleas of the people before God. So, Jesus isn't just Lord who sits ruling and reigning far off, but He is our representative. Scripture says that He sympathizes with our weaknesses in that role. He offers Himself as the final sacrifice for sin, and He is our mediator before God the Father, presenting our prayers and requests before Him.

So, when we think about Jesus, it's important that we don't box Him in or make Him too small. He is King, so we worship Him and pray to Him because He has the power to do all things. But He is also our Priest, so we worship Him and pray to Him because He is wonderfully empathetic and caring, and has paid the price for our rebellion Himself.

Our King is a Priest, and our Priest is a King. Praise Him.

Prayer:

Father God, thank you for the magnificent gift of your son, Jesus. Teach us to trust in His rule and reign in our lives, and teach us to believe in His empathy as our representative.

Psalm 111

Smart Obedience

Reading:

Read the entire psalm, and then read the following verse again.

> *The fear of the LORD is the beginning of wisdom;*
> > *all those who practice it have a good understanding.*
> *His praise endures forever!*
> > *Psalm 111:10*

Reflection:

I grew up with a warped image of God. It was of my own making by and large. I believed somehow that God was something of a cosmic killjoy who took great delight in telling His kids that they could not do any of the things that looked like the most fun.

Sex—You can't do that. It would be too much fun.
Partying—Nope.
Fun again.
Drinking a lot—No chance. Fun.

Of course, when you view God like that, you are automatically drawn to all the things you can't do, like a moth to a flame. I already see a lot of this in my son Daniel. As soon as I tell him he can't do something, he is tempted to do it, even if he wasn't considering doing it before I told him he couldn't. Suddenly, it looks like massive fun.

The Psalmist tells us in Psalm 111 that wisdom comes when we obey God. The smartest people on the planet are the ones who have figured out that God's precepts, principles, and commands are not there to steal our joy, but they are there to protect our joy and save us from our own destruction. He tells us not to do certain things because those things ruin us. He tells us to do other things because doing those things makes us more alive.

He is no killjoy; rather, He is a "give-joy." But only the smartest people realize it.

Be smart today. Obey God. In a world that equates wisdom with rebellion, be wise through obedience.

Prayer:

Father God, teach me to trust you so that I know your ways are the ways that lead to life and joy and flourishing. Forgive me for the many ways I choose less than that. Show me areas where I am currently failing to trust in your wisdom, and help me to trust you in those areas.

Psalm 112

Mastering Money

Reading:

Read the entire psalm, and then read the following verses again.

> ⁵ *It is well with the man who deals generously and lends;*
> *who conducts his affairs with justice.*
> ⁶ *For the righteous will never be moved;*
> *he will be remembered forever.*
> ⁷ *He is not afraid of bad news;*
> *his heart is firm, trusting in the LORD.*
> ⁸ *His heart is steady; he will not be afraid,*
> *until he looks in triumph on his adversaries.*
> ⁹ *He has distributed freely; he has given to the poor;*
> *his righteousness endures forever;*
> *his horn is exalted in honor.*
> *Psalm 112:5–9*

Reflection:

Psalm 112 looks at the life of a blessed person who is righteous with their wealth. It seems to me that when I read the Scriptures, God is less concerned with whether we are wealthy or poor than He is with whether we are righteous or unrighteous with the wealth we have. Now, it is true that there are warnings for those who have wealth (Luke 6:24; James 5:1), but wealth is something that comes with warnings, rather than something that is forbidden.

What, then, is the biblical instruction given to people when it comes to money? The two big things that the Bible calls us to are contentment and generosity. The blessed man in Psalm 112 isn't afraid of bad news and isn't easily moved in his heart. He is content and not living beyond his means. 1 Timothy 6:6–10 tells us,

> But godliness with contentment is great gain, for we brought nothing into the world, and we cannot take anything out of the world. But if we have food and clothing, with these we will be content. But those who desire to be rich fall into temptation, into a snare, into many senseless and harmful desires that plunge people into ruin and destruction. For the love of money is a root of all kinds of evils. It is through this craving that some have wandered away from the faith and pierced themselves with many pangs.

When Paul quotes this psalm in 2 Corinthians 9:6-9 and following, he uses it to call us to not just contentment, but to extreme generosity that speaks of the generosity of the gospel. He says,

> The point is this: whoever sows sparingly will also reap sparingly, and whoever sows bountifully will also reap bountifully. Each one must give as he has decided in his heart, not reluctantly or under compulsion, for God loves a cheerful giver. And God is able to make all grace abound to you, so that having all sufficiency in all things at all times, you may abound in every good work. As it is written,

"He has distributed freely, he has given to
the poor; his righteousness endures forever."

So, how are you doing with money? Are you able to display the righteous fruits of contentment and generosity? Do the things you have fought so hard to own now end up owning you?

Prayer:

Father God, everything I have is yours. You have been so good to me. Teach me to be a righteous steward of the resources you have trusted me with. Free me, God, from the love of money.

Psalm 113

God Stoops Low

Reading:

Read the entire psalm, and then read the following verses again.

> [7] *He raises the poor from the dust*
>   *and lifts the needy from the ash heap,*
> [8] *to make them sit with princes,*
>   *with the princes of his people.*
>   *Psalm 113:7–8*

Reflection:

Psalm 113 is a psalm of praise. It speaks of God being higher than the heavens, seated on a throne, far beyond the reach of those on earth. This is how we imagine those with great power. Lifted up, out of reach, up above.

But the psalm tells the beautiful tale of the love of the God of the Bible. We have no way at all to reach up to Him, but He stoops down to the lowly. He gets in and amongst the poor and the unlovely, and He lifts them up to be with Him.

Two things come to my mind with this reminder. First, I am so grateful that God stooped low in the form of His Son to come and get a poor soul like me. I mustn't give in to the thinking that I ascended up to God, even for a moment. Second, if this is the impulse of God, then I am called as His follower to do what I can to lift up the lowly and bring out the poor from the dust.

When was the last time you contemplated God's mercy toward you and believed that you can't reach up to Him, but that He reached down to you? When was the last time you celebrated God's mercy toward you by extending mercy toward another?

Prayer:

Father God, thank you that you stooped low to get me. Give me eyes to see and hands to help those who need lifting up. Send me as an agent of your mercy toward those who need mercy.

Psalm 114

Nothing Can Stop Us

Reading:

Read the entire psalm, and then read the following verses again.

> ⁵ *What ails you, O sea, that you flee?*
>   *O Jordan, that you turn back?*
> ⁶ *O mountains, that you skip like rams?*
>   *O hills, like lambs?*
> ⁷ *Tremble, O earth, at the presence of the* LORD,
>   *at the presence of the God of Jacob,*
> ⁸ *who turns the rock into a pool of water,*
>   *the flint into a spring of water.*
>   *Psalm 114:5–8*

Reflection:

One of the previous preaching series at our church, called "Follow," dealt with four qualities that disciples of Jesus should have in increasing measure if they are to mature and multiply. It was a profound time of self-examination for us as a church. The four qualities we discussed were:

- Rooted in the Gospel
- Empowered by the Spirit
- Living in Community
- Working on Mission

It struck me this morning that Psalm 114 is actually a great summary of the series.

The psalm begins by praising God for the fact that He delivered Israel out of slavery. He took them from darkness to light, and from oppression to freedom. He does the same thing for us today, and it is all accomplished by Him. We just respond to this freedom by living like free men. When we live in a way that displays that freedom, then we show that we are rooted in the gospel.

Second, the psalm speaks of how God dwelt with the people of Israel. He lived with them. He still does the same thing today for His saints; in fact, He does even better and now dwells in His people and not amongst them. Followers of Christ aren't left to try and follow Christ on their own strength, but they are gifted the supernatural power of the Holy Spirit of God to transform them and empower them. In order to get this power, all they need to do is ask. Maybe that is a great reminder today: just ask. That is living empowered by the Spirit.

Third, God made Israel into a new kind of people. They numbered a couple of million, but the Psalmist refers to them as one family. They were totally unified by what God had done for them and in them. The same is supposed to be true of the church today. We are called to be a community and not a corporation. We are supposed to be a family and not an institution. When people truly get that, they are redeemed and empowered. They no longer have to pretend, and the things that unite them are far more powerful than the things that divide them. That is genuine dwelling in community.

Last, the Psalmist speaks powerfully and poetically of how God led His people into a new land, and how even creation stood back in awe as God went with His people on their new mission. The redeemed have always been called to restore, and God has always promised to go with redeemed restorers. I hope that is a great reminder to you today—that God is with you as you go, and that not even seas or mountains or rocks can stand in the way of God in you when you go. That is mission to live for.

How are you growing in these four areas as a disciple of Jesus?

Prayer:

Father God, remind me, oh God, how the earth trembles at your presence. Give me a deep desire to become more like your Son, and help me grow in these areas as I pursue that end by your power and grace.

Psalm 115

Trusting in the Temporary

Reading:

Take time to read the entire psalm, and then read the following verses again.

> [4] *Their idols are silver and gold,*
>   *the work of human hands.*
> [5] *They have mouths, but do not speak;*
>   *eyes, but do not see.*
> [6] *They have ears, but do not hear;*
>   *noses, but do not smell.*
> [7] *They have hands, but do not feel;*
>   *feet, but do not walk;*
>   *and they do not make a sound in their throat.*
> [8] *Those who make them become like them;*
>   *so do all who trust in them.*
>   *Psalm 115:4–8*

Reflection:

Psalm 115 serves as a stark warning against our tendency toward idolatry. The notion of worshipping a God that is so much larger than us is difficult for our self-obsessed souls to deal with, and so again and again we make things that we can give worship, affections, and sacrifice to. It gives us a feeling of control back, when worship is really supposed to take that feeling away. The problem is, as the Psalmist warns us, we end up becoming as lifeless as the lifeless things we worship. True worship of a living God leads to life and truth. False worship of a dead idea leads to death and deceit.

So, what are you giving your worship to? Let me ask it another way: what gets your trust, your affections, your sacrifice, your attention? The temporal things that we love to turn to will turn on us. Don't give them your worship.

Prayer:

Father God, we echo the prayer of the Psalmist and say, "Not to us, O LORD, not to us, but to your name give glory, for the sake of your steadfast love and your faithfulness!"

Psalm 116

Precious Death

Reading:

Read the entire psalm, and then read the following verse again.

> *Precious in the sight of the LORD*
> *is the death of his saints.*
> *Psalm 116:15*

Reflection:

Some time ago, I had the rare privilege of conducting the memorial service of a family member. We loved her very much and it was a tough day, full of all the emotion associated with remembering a shared past, and considering an unshared future.

Yet this memorial had a sense of victory in the mourning, a sense of triumph in the tears, a sense of certainty in the confusion.

Why? Was it a vain hope, or a series of empty platitudes in an attempt to provide short-term comfort? I don't think so. I think it was because many of the people in the room believed the Bible, and what it says about death for those who believe.

My relative was a saint, and when I say that, I don't mean she was very good—I mean she was a saint in the biblical sense, which means she was a forgiven daughter of God. The Bible says that God isn't indifferent when one of His saints dies. In fact, the Psalmist tells us that He considers it a precious occasion.

Precious? How?

John caught a glimpse of this in Revelation. He was shown a vision of heaven, and then was instructed by the Holy Spirit:

> "Write this: Blessed are the dead who die in the LORD from now on."
> "Yes," says the Spirit, "they will rest from their labor, for their deeds will follow them."
>
> Revelation 14:13 (NIV)

Saints receive rest when they die, so God sees it as precious because He knows how hard life has been. As a loving God, He enjoys being able to welcome His saints into a state of rest. No more strife, doubt, sickness, suffering, struggle, or pain. Just rest.

Saints receive reward when they die, so God sees it as precious because as a loving dad He wants to lavish undeserved gifts on His kids. No more earning, striving, saving, and wondering if we are good enough. Just lavish grace and reward.

When I ponder these things, two things start to happen. First, I start to identify with Paul more and more, as he said, "To die is gain." I get it. Death for the saint is better, by far. But I also start to understand what he meant when he said, "To live is Christ," because if this stuff is true, then I want to use every available breath I have to let as many as possible know what it takes and what it means to be a saint, and what awaits those who are.

Prayer:

Father God, my death will one day be precious in your sight. Teach me to live for Christ so that on that day, those left behind will have a great deal of hope in their mourning.

Sometimes You Can Say More with Fewer Words

Reading:

Read the entire psalm, and then read it over again.

> ¹ *Praise the* L<small>ORD</small>*, all nations!*
>   *Extol him, all peoples!*
> ² *For great is his steadfast love toward us,*
>   *and the faithfulness of the* L<small>ORD</small> *endures forever.*
> *Praise the* L<small>ORD</small>*!*
>
> *Psalm 117:1-2*

Reflection:

Psalm 117 is seventeen words long in the Hebrew. It is by far the shortest of the Psalms, yet it contains a really meaningful sentiment. The Psalmist declares that God is loving, good, caring, and worthy of praise, regardless of individual circumstances. In other words, we do well when we view our circumstances through the lenses of the known character of God, rather than viewing God through the blurry lenses of our circumstances.

We may respond by saying, "Well, that's easy for you to say; you don't know what I am going through." That's true, but most commentators agree that this psalm is post-exilic, which means it was written just after Israel had gone through the roughest season of its history. They had been enslaved, tortured, dehumanized, and many of them killed. They had experienced suffering to a level few of us could ever even imagine, yet, "The faithfulness of the Lord endures forever."

Maybe your circumstances mean that you don't have many words right now. That's okay. But if you can use your few words to testify to the fact that God is loving and faithful, then your big God will dwarf your small circumstances, and joy will come.

Prayer:

Spend some time in silence before the Lord. Think and reflect on His goodness and kindness toward you. Then pray.

Psalm 118

The Truth at the Center

Reading:

Read the entire psalm, and then read the following verses again.

> [6] *The LORD is on my side; I will not fear.*
>   *What can man do to me?*
> [7] *The LORD is on my side as my helper;*
>   *I shall look in triumph on those who hate me.*
> [8] *It is better to take refuge in the LORD*
>   *than to trust in man.*
> [9] *It is better to take refuge in the LORD*
>   *than to trust in princes.*
>   *Psalm 118:6–9*

Reflection:

In his masterful work on the Psalms, Spurgeon notes—in almost a throwaway line—that many scholars contest that verse 8 of Psalm 118 is the very center point of the Bible in terms of number of verses. If there are 31,174 verses in the Bible, then Psalm 118:8 is verse number 15,587. Spurgeon goes on to suggest that shouldn't give this undue attention, and I agree. We don't need to get into superstitious numerology, and, besides, the verse numbers were only allocated much later than the sealing of the canon.

But for the sake of this devotion, I can't help but dwell a bit on this simple verse that sits right at the middle of it all. It really is such a simple truth that it belongs in the middle.

> It is better to take refuge in the LORD
> than to trust in man.

Martin Luther called this discipline (taking refuge in the Lord) "the art of arts" and the "most pleasing and pleasant of sacrifices." So, the question to us today is, are we holding to this simple truth at the center of our faith? Are you trusting God or trusting men? Are you relying on God or depending on people for affirmation, identity, and salvation?

At the center of it all is a plea to fear God and to not fear anyone else. Will we listen?

It is better to take refuge in the Lord. Do it.

Prayer:

Father God, forgive me for the many ways I trust in mankind more than I trust in you. Teach me to fear you, and then relieve me of the fear I have of everyone else.

Not Who I Should Be, but Not Who I Used to Be

Reading:

Try to take the time to read the entire psalm. It is long, but worth it. When you are done, read the following verses again.

> ¹ Blessed are those whose way is blameless,
>   who walk in the law of the LORD!
> ² Blessed are those who keep his testimonies,
>   who seek him with their whole heart,
> ³ who also do no wrong,
>   but walk in his ways!
> ⁴ You have commanded your precepts
>   to be kept diligently.
> ⁵ Oh that my ways may be steadfast
>   in keeping your statutes!
> ⁶ Then I shall not be put to shame,
>   having my eyes fixed on all your commandments.
> ⁷ I will praise you with an upright heart,
>   when I learn your righteous rules.
> ⁸ I will keep your statutes;
>   do not utterly forsake me!
>   *Psalm 119:1–8*

Reflection:

Psalm 119 is the longest of the Psalms at 166 verses, so there are quite a few themes to reflect on as you read it. I have to confess to having grown despondent when I began to reflect on it, though. The first four verses were pretty discouraging to me, as they describe a type of man who isn't like me. He is blameless in all he does, and he keeps the law of the Lord perfectly. He seeks God with all his heart, all the time, and never does anything wrong. The Psalmist says that kind of guy is blessed, but, unfortunately, I'm not that kind of guy, and I don't know anyone who is.

I tend to seek my own desired outcomes more than I seek the Lord. My actions and thoughts couldn't be said to leave me blameless. I cannot say I don't do anything wrong: in fact, I often find I am drawn to what is wrong, like a moth to the proverbial flame. It is not all bad. Christ is changing me, to be sure, but if the standard is the first four verses of Psalm 119—well then, quite frankly I am in a fair deal of trouble.

Praise God for the arrival of verse 5. Praise God for the honesty of the Bible. The Psalmist declares he doesn't live up to the standard: he cries out in prayer for greater steadfastness. In so doing, he openly acknowledges that he fails, but he is also hopeful that he is in process. He is learning, and so am I, praise God.

So be at peace today as you read Psalm 119. If you are walking with God, then you are blameless even if your actions and thoughts aren't because of the righteousness of Christ. That knowledge has the power to change you as you learn to walk in righteousness.

Prayer:

Oh, Lord, I pray that you would keep me steadfast. I don't want to be put to shame. Teach me to follow you and your truth more faithfully, and thank you that you aren't done with me yet.

Psalm 120

Don't Waste Your Dysfunction

Reading:

Read the entire psalm, and then read the following verse again.

> *In my distress I called to the LORD,*
> *and he answered me.*
> *Psalm 120:1*

Reflection:

A desire for self-improvement is ingrained into the human experience. It is a good thing that we want to be better versions of ourselves. It can become problematic, though, when we start to feel like the future version of ourselves will be the thing that is lovable by others and by God. I speak to a lot of people who have a deep desire to walk closely with God but who feel that their current dysfunction disqualifies them from getting that relationship going. "Let me just get this sorted out, and then God and I will talk," is a sentiment I hear way too often, and even one I find myself believing.

Psalm 120 is a strange passage of Scripture. The Psalmist was isolated, lonely, rejected, and desirous of vengeance. He didn't exactly have it all together, but...he called to the Lord, and the Lord answered him.

Don't wait 'til you have it all together. Don't believe the lie that says that God is waiting for a more palatable version of you to interact with. Call out to Him. He loves the dysfunctional. Trust me.

Prayer:

Father God, thank you so much for the knowledge that you don't only love and accept a future, improved version of me. I can cry out to you now, and you will hear. So, I will.

Psalm 121

Eyes Up

Reading:

Read the entire psalm, and then read the following verses again.

> *¹ I lift up my eyes to the hills.*
> *From where does my help come?*
> *² My help comes from the LORD,*
> *who made heaven and earth.*
> *Psalm 121:1–2*

Reflection:

When I was a kid, I took part in a multi-day hike in the Blyde River Canyon. It is a majestic and intimidating place, full of beauty but also full of peril and hard work. One of the things about hiking through a canyon is that you can get quite easily disoriented. The steep canyon walls begin to press in on you, and it can start to feel like you are making no progress and that you may have no way out of the valley's vice grip. The antidote to this is to climb and get to higher ground where you can get another perspective on your progress and the landscape.

This is what Psalm 121 is about: lifting your eyes from the pressing intensity of your current circumstances so that you can get better perspective on who is actually in charge of the universe. I love what Spurgeon said in his commentary on this psalm: "It is wise to look to the strong for strength. Dwellers in valleys are subject to many disorders for which there is no cure but a sojourn in the uplands, and it is well when they shake off their lethargy and resolve upon a climb."[20]

So, where are you looking to for your hope? Lift your eyes. Look to the hills, and move forward. Spend some time lifting your eyes to the truth of God, and then bring your circumstances to Him with that view in mind.

Prayer:

Dear Lord, teach me to lift my eyes and look to you. When I look at things around me, I get discouraged. Give me an understanding of how you are ruling from above, and let that bring me strength and courage and hope.

---

20. Spurgeon, *The Treasury of David, Volume 3: Part 2*, 14.

Psalm 122

Glad in God

Reading:

Read the entire psalm, and then read the following verse again.

> *I was glad when they said to me,*
> *"Let us go to the house of the LORD!"*
> *Psalm 122:1*

Reflection:

Psalm 122 seems at first read to be a celebration of the city of Jerusalem. Although, a little research shows us that David is celebrating more than just the city. He wrote this psalm just after the Ark of the Covenant had been recovered and brought into Jerusalem. So, what David is celebrating in Psalm 122 is the presence of God among His people.

God with men. What a thought.

One of the glories of the gospel is that God now dwells in and with His saints. We don't need to contain Him in a physical building in a literal city, as He has taken up residence in us, and so is transforming us into temples for His precious and wonderful Holy Spirit.

The question for us, then, is does that knowledge make us glad? David was elated at the thought of God's presence, yet I so often take it for granted and fail to live in the full reality of the glorious availability of the presence of the living God to little old me. Why wouldn't I want more of that? Why wouldn't the very notion make us elated like David?

The thing is that we are forgetful beasts, so we go back to the old way of things all the time. We gravitate toward self-sufficiency. Here are some practical tips to help remind us of the availability of the glorious presence of God in our lives.

1. Prayer. We all want to pray more than we do, but most of us get intimidated when we think of carving out hours of our day to be on our knees. I have started to fill downtime in my day with prayer, so I pray in my car, I pray in the shower, I pray in staff meetings, I pray in the line at the grocery store, I try to just pray all the time. The key to this is to remember that prayer doesn't need to be an attempt to impress anyone with cleverness, but it should be a conversation with your heavenly dad. The more I pray, the more I feel the joy that comes with His unmistakable presence.

2. Scripture. I know this is predictable from a pastor, but reading the Bible really does help us experience God. Don't try to read the whole thing at once, and use technology to help you if you need it. Just read this precious thing.

3. Corporate Worship. David uses plural language as he speaks about the joy of being able to engage with God's presence. Something special happens when God's people get together and declare truths about Him. Be a regular at church gatherings. Try to get there early, and try to really think through the words we sing. If they speak of a physical response (e.g., I lift my hands), then do it. Spend time praying in the car on the way to church, asking God to speak to you and reveal Himself to you. Be deliberate about it, instead of just arriving.

4. Asking. The scandal of the requirement for us to receive God's Spirit is astounding. Just ask. That's it. God gives to those who ask for the Holy Spirit. I have started to make it a daily request from God: "Lord, please fill me with your Holy Spirit."

I pray that through some of these measures we might become people who take great delight in the presence of God.

Prayer:

Father God, fill me with your Holy Spirit, and make me glad.

Psalm 123

Saved to Serve

Reading:

Read the entire psalm, and then read the following verses again.

> ¹ *To you I lift up my eyes,*
>   *O you who are enthroned in the heavens!*
> ² *Behold, as the eyes of servants*
>   *look to the hand of their master,*
>   *as the eyes of a maidservant*
>   *to the hand of her mistress,*
>   *so our eyes look to the* LORD *our God,*
>   *till he has mercy upon us.*
>   *Psalm 123:1–2*

Reflection:

I make a terrible God. Seriously, things are most difficult in my life when I forget where I fit. When I place myself subconsciously as the ruler and judge of my own life, things don't go all that well. My anxiety increases and my peace and joy decrease, probably because I am trying to play a role I was never built to play.

In Psalm 123, the Psalmist reminds us where we fit. He describes us as loving servants looking up toward our master and awaiting instructions. In biblical times, servants were part of the family unit. They were welcomed into every part of the functioning of the home, but they were also so integrated into the home that the whole purpose of their life was to please their master.

They lived to serve.

The Bible is full of verses speaking about God loving us and making us part of His family. That is all true and wonderful, but we have a propensity for overestimating the role we have to play when we think that being part of the family means that we get to call the shots. We don't.

I can honestly say I am most joyful when I am most trusting.

I am most peaceful when I am most submissive.

I am most satisfied when I am most servant-hearted.

Try it for a bit.

Remind yourself daily that you are a servant. Align your life with that, and assess your current circumstances in the light of that knowledge.

You are saved to serve. You were bought with a price. Enjoy it.

Prayer:

Father God, remind me today and from this day forward that I exist to serve you. Bring me the peace that comes from the clarity of that purpose and position.

Psalm 124

Team Jesus

Reading:

Read the entire psalm, and then read the following verses again.

> ¹ *If it had not been the* LORD *who was on our side—*
>   *let Israel now say—*
> ² *if it had not been the* LORD *who was on our side*
>   *when people rose up against us,*
> ³ *then they would have swallowed us up alive,*
>   *when their anger was kindled against us;*
> ⁴ *then the flood would have swept us away,*
>   *the torrent would have gone over us;*
> ⁵ *then over us would have gone*
>   *the raging waters.*
>   *Psalm 124:1–5*

Reflection:

Can we really say that God is on our side? I know we say that all the time, but can we—and should we? It seems ridiculous to me when sports stars thank God for helping them win, and when living-large musicians and actors publically thank God for being on their side. What about those who don't make it to the Academy Awards? What about the other team? Was God opposed to them? And is God really interested in the results of sports matches and award ceremonies?

Because this can look so silly, I have tended to veer away from thinking of a God that chooses sides, but this can ultimately lead to me thinking that I am on my own in the world and the struggles I encounter in it. That doesn't feel right or biblical, either.

In Psalm 124, David looked both backwards and forwards, and came to the conclusion that God was definitely with him. He looked back at ways he and the people had been delivered, and it was obvious to him that it wouldn't have worked out that way if God hadn't been with them and for them. He also looked forward prophetically to the day it would be obvious that God was with His people.

That day has already come. When Jesus came to the world to rescue us, He declared that He would be with us forever. As Matthew Henry said while commenting on this psalm:

"God was on our side; he took our part, espoused our cause and appeared for us. He was our helper, and a very present help, a help on our side, nigh at hand. He was with us; not only for us, but among us, and commander-in-chief of our forces."[21]

This led me to consider afresh one of the most popular and most profound texts in all of Scripture. Read it slowly, without assuming you know what it says:

> [28]And we know that for those who love God all things work together for good, for those who are called according to his purpose. [29]For those whom he foreknew he also predestined to be conformed to the image of his Son, in order that he might be the firstborn among many brothers. [30]And those whom he predestined he also called, and those whom he called he also justified,

---

21. Matthew Henry, *"Matthew Henry's Commentary on the Whole Bible"* (Peabody, MA: Hendrickson Publishers, 2000), 931.

and those whom he justified he also glorified.[31] What then shall we say to these things? If God is for us, who can be against us?[32] He who did not spare his own Son but gave him up for us all, how will he not also with him graciously give us all things?[33] Who shall bring any charge against God's elect? It is God who justifies.[34] Who is to condemn? Christ Jesus is the one who died—more than that, who was raised—who is at the right hand of God, who indeed is interceding for us.[35] Who shall separate us from the love of Christ? Shall tribulation, or distress, or persecution, or famine, or nakedness, or danger, or sword?[36] As it is written,

> "For your sake we are being killed all the
> day long; we are regarded as sheep to be
> slaughtered."

[37]No, in all these things we are more than conquerors through him who loved us.[38] For I am sure that neither death nor life, nor angels nor rulers, nor things present nor things to come, nor powers,[39] nor height nor depth, nor anything else in all creation, will be able to separate us from the love of God in Christ Jesus our Lord.

Romans 8:28–39

The only one who can condemn us intercedes for us. The only one who can judge us, saves us. The only one we really need to fear as an adversary is on our side. Now, that provides some much-needed courage for today.

Team Jesus? You bet.

Prayer:

Father God, if you weren't for us, we really would be in trouble. Give us faith and courage to believe you are for us through your Son, and to live lives of fearless worship knowing that you are for us.

Psalm 125

Feeling Surrounded?

Reading:

Read the entire psalm, and then read the following verse again.

> *As the mountains surround Jerusalem,*
> *so the L*ORD *surrounds his people,*
> *from this time forth and forevermore.*
> *Psalm 125:2*

Reflection:

My parents live in a city in the USA called Boise, Idaho. It is a beautiful place that has its own issues, to be sure, but I love hanging out there. The city is located in an old volcanic bowl, so it is surrounded completely by snow-capped mountains. Wherever you are in the city, and in whatever direction you are looking, you can see the mountains looking back at you. It is weirdly comforting to feel totally surrounded.

The Psalmist says that God surrounds His people just like mountains surround a city. I love this image. It means that no matter which way I look, God is there.

If I look behind me, He is there, covering all my past sin and rebellion, and with the blessing of hindsight I am able to see He was guiding me all along.

If I look in front of me, He is there, guiding my future and leading me toward His plans for my life. I don't have to fear what is in front of me, because He is there.

If I look to the side, He is there, hedging me in and making sure I don't stray too far from the path.

So, whatever you are facing today—and I know you may be facing a lot—remember that you are surrounded by your loving Father who is watching over you.

Prayer:

Father God, give me eyes to see how you have surrounded me with your love, your presence, your mercy, and your faithfulness.

Psalm 126

Daydreaming

Reading:

Read the entire psalm, and then read the following verses again.

> ¹ When the LORD restored the fortunes of Zion,
>   we were like those who dream.
> ² Then our mouth was filled with laughter,
>   and our tongue with shouts of joy;
>   then they said among the nations,
>   "The LORD has done great things for them."
> ³ The LORD has done great things for us;
>   we are glad.
>
> *Psalm 126:1–3*

Reflection:

As people we are usually very quick to cry out to God for intervention and pretty slow to cry out to God for thanksgiving, even when it is clear He has intervened.

I can't help myself today, though. Just like the Psalmist, I feel like I am living a dream.

God has been so faithful to me and to the people I get to serve that I am simply overwhelmed and overjoyed at His care and love He so relentlessly extends toward us.

I just pray that we take the time to notice. We can become so obsessed with what we haven't seen that we don't stop to have appropriate awe at what we have seen.

How about you? On reflection, how kind has God been toward you and your people?

> The LORD has done great things for us;
> we are glad.

Indeed.

Take time today to write down some of the many things God has done for you. Practice an exercise of thanksgiving and let that determine the tone of the rest of your day.

Prayer:

Father God, today we come before you not to ask you for anything, but simply to thank you for your kindness and grace toward us. Thank you for your mercy. Thank you for your love. Thank you, Lord.

Psalm 127

Don't Waste Your Life

Reading:

Read the entire psalm, and then read the following verses again.

> ¹ Unless the LORD builds the house,
>   those who build it labor in vain.
>   Unless the LORD watches over the city,
>   the watchman stays awake in vain.
> ² It is in vain that you rise up early
>   and go late to rest,
>   eating the bread of anxious toil;
>   for he gives to his beloved sleep.
>   Psalm 127:1–2

Reflection:

Many of the scholars agree that Psalm 127 was most likely written by David about and for his son Solomon, as Solomon was tasked to build the temple of the Lord in Jerusalem. When read in this light, it is a reminder for us to live toward what God has called us to do. David had a desperate desire to build the temple. He wanted a legacy left for Israel that would make his life matter in spiritual terms, but God denied him that privilege and rather promised David that his offspring would be the one who would get to do it. David knew that there was no way to overrule or change that, so he speaks from first-hand knowledge when we warns Solomon that no amount of toiling and laboring will amount to anything if it isn't done according to the will and purposes of God.

How many of us live in a Psalm 127:2 reality, though? Up early, in bed late, working hard to buy stuff, and then buying stuff because we have worked hard, but struggling to sleep because we know that the Lord isn't in the center of what we are building? We know from the rest of Scripture that God isn't opposed to us working hard, but we see clearly here that if it isn't done with God at the center, it is done in vain.

When was the last time you actually asked God what He wanted from your life? When was the last time you actually relinquished control to Him in terms of what you are building?

Take some time now to again set God's purposes above your own. Please, friend, don't waste your life.

Prayer:

Father God, unless you build it, it will collapse, and I know that. Forgive me for building furiously anyway. Show me the things I am building in vain, and teach me to wait for you and to listen to you, so that I build what you want.

Psalm 128

Growing Grace at Home

Reading:

Read the entire psalm, and then read the following verses again.

> *¹ Blessed is everyone who fears the LORD,*
> *who walks in his ways!*
> *² You shall eat the fruit of the labor of your hands;*
> *you shall be blessed, and it shall be well with you.*
> *³ Your wife will be like a fruitful vine*
> *within your house;*
> *your children will be like olive shoots*
> *around your table.*
> *Psalm 128:1–3*

Reflection:

Psalm 128 is a powerful poem that should be ingrained into the heart and mind of every man who is a husband and a father, or desires to be one. It speaks of the kind of environment that a godly man can nurture so that his wife and children can flourish freely in his home.[22]

---

22. I know and understand that there are godly homes and family units that don't have dads and husbands present. We applaud the work of single moms and cheer you on. This devotion isn't meant to exclude you, in any way.

It speaks of the wife as a fruitful vine. She is well-established and enjoying room for growth and development without fear of being cut down. It speaks of children who are like olive shoots. They are tender and delicate, but hopeful and full of potential for something beautiful. So how does a man create the kind of environment where his wife and children can grow like this? The man is obviously not the sole creator of home environments, but as the head of the family he must work with his family and not over them in trying to create this kind of space.

1. He sets the spiritual tone. Psalm 128 is actually more about a man who follows God than anything else. The environment in his home is consequential of the divine priorities that he displays. Men, be the most passionate pursuer of Christ in your home. It will provide a great deal of comfort, excitement, and faith for your wife and kids if they see you on your knees frequently.

2. He cultivates growth. Vines don't grow by accident, and neither do olive shoots. They need to be fed, watered, nurtured, and cared for in order for them to be healthy. Men, your words can raise people up or cut them down. Are you doing all you can to raise up and nurture your wife and kids? You are the mood architect of your home. Is your home a place of free and joyful growth, or is it a scary place where people are frightened to fail because they have been cut down before?

3. He roots out the pests. Anyone who has ever tried to grow anything knows that there are a number of pests you have to guard against in order to ensure healthy and sustainable growth. Here are three pests that may well be eating away at the growth in your home.
    i.   Discontentment. Many people feel unhappy and unsatisfied with their lot, and as a man this discontent can creep into resentment toward the wife Christ has given him and the

kids he has been blessed with. Stop peering over the wall at a greener-looking yard and start to enjoy the immense blessing you already have. Let your wife know she is the best thing that ever happened to you, and let your kids know your life got significantly better when they arrived and that you wouldn't have it any other way.

ii.   Distraction. This is a big one and one I fight daily. I really want my son to see my face more than he sees the back of my iPhone. Turn the phone off. Turn the TV off. Eat at the table. Ask your kids about their day, and then listen intently to whatever they say.

iii. Discouragement. Does your wife feel gorgeous? Do your kids feel encouraged? Men, it isn't enough for your family to assume how you feel about them. Tell them often. Show them continually. Write love letters to your wife and take your kids on surprise outings with no agenda. Be the engineer of fun, spontaneity, and encouragement in your home.

I am praying for loving homes where wives are free to grow and flourish and where kids feel loved, safe, secure, and comforted. Go be the men that can make that happen.

Prayer:

Father God, we long for homes that speak of your goodness and your kindness to a world that desperately needs to hear of that and see it in action. Teach us to be cultivators of these sorts of homes.

Psalm 129

Cutting the Cords

Reading:

Read the entire psalm, and then read the following verses again.

> ² *"Greatly have they afflicted me from my youth,*
> *yet they have not prevailed against me.*
> ³ *The plowers plowed upon my back;*
> *they made long their furrows."*
> ⁴ *The LORD is righteous;*
> *he has cut the cords of the wicked.*
> ⁵ *May all who hate Zion*
> *be put to shame and turned backward!*
> *Psalm 129:2–5*

Reflection:

Psalm 129 is part of a sub-section of the Psalms known as "The Songs of Ascent." There is a lot of mystery and a fair deal of myth around these psalms and their place in the worship practices of Israel. What does seem clear, though, is that they speak of the return of the presence of God to His people and the songs that should be sung as the ascent to His holy hill is made. With that in mind, Psalm 129 is a strange addition. We expect songs of high and holy declarations of triumph, yet here is an acknowledgement that enemies have plagued the Psalmist since his youth. Psalm 129 is a prayer that God would release him from what seems to have been a lifelong torment.

I am deeply encouraged that Psalm 129 makes it into this song book. All too often, I am reminded of the things that have plagued me from my youth. Temptations, obstacles, prevailing sins, doubts, wrestles. I often feel like I have to pretend to not have those if I am going to ascend the "holy hill of the Lord." Psalm 129 reminds me:

> Greatly have they afflicted me from my youth,
>   yet they have not prevailed against me.

I can ascend. I can look up. My struggles won't prevail against me forever. God has cut those cords.

Prayer:

Father God, give me eyes to see how you have cut the cords that feel like they continue to restrain and bind me. I long to ascend. Help me fix my eyes on you and believe in your grace and your mercy.

Psalm 130

Fear and Forgiveness

Reading:

Read the entire psalm, and then read the following verses again.

> *3 If you, O LORD, should mark iniquities,*
>   *O LORD, who could stand?*
> *4 But with you there is forgiveness,*
>   *that you may be feared.*
>   *Psalm 130:3–4*

Reflection:

At some point when I was in high school, it was decided that allowing relative strangers to spank teenage boys was no longer acceptable. They needed then to institute a new disciplinary system, so the idea of merits and demerits came about. If you did something extraordinarily good (like bringing about world peace), you got a merit, and if you did anything wrong (like looking vaguely uninterested in Latin class), you got a demerit. The idea was that if you got too far into the negatives, bad things would happen; and if you did well in the racking-up of merits, good stuff could abound for you. I think they got the idea from Santa Claus, to be honest.

It ended up being a ridiculously fruitless system open to much manipulation, yet it's exactly how many of us think the universe runs. As if God is a cruel headmaster overseeing horribly outdated rules and scoring us with merits and demerits, and in the end we have a deep hope that the merits will be the winners and good will abound for us. In the meanwhile, we should just stay out of God's way, because He is probably mad at us for all the fun we are having.

The problem with seeing God that way is the Bible. In fact, Psalm 130 tells us that if God ran the universe this way, we would all be in big trouble. No one would score enough merits. No one could stand before a holy God if He was keeping score.

Praise God for verse 4. Our God is a God of forgiveness. He doesn't keep score but pays all the demerits through His innocent Son. My school teachers would have thought this kind of grace would have led to mass chaos and anarchy, yet the Psalmist seems to think that it leads to greater reverence, respect, awe, and worship. The fact that God isn't keeping score on my obedience really makes me want to obey Him, because He is wonderful.

Believe in Him. Be quick to repent. Be quick to forgive. If He isn't keeping score, you really shouldn't be.

Prayer:

Father God, thank you so much that through the righteousness of your Son, I am merited with perfect righteousness. Give me faith to believe that, and boldness and wisdom to live like it is true.

Psalm 131

The Glory of Knowing What You Don't Know

Reading:

Take the time to read this short psalm a couple of times.

> *¹ O LORD, my heart is not lifted up;*
> *my eyes are not raised too high;*
> *I do not occupy myself with things*
> *too great and too marvelous for me.*
> *² But I have calmed and quieted my soul,*
> *like a weaned child with its mother;*
> *like a weaned child is my soul within me.*
>
> *³ O Israel, hope in the LORD*
> *from this time forth and forevermore.*
> *Psalm 131:1–3*

Reflection:

Psalm 131 is David at his finest. He is honest, vulnerable, and humble, but still full of faith. I reckon we can learn a lot from him (well, I can anyway).

Some days you don't feel on top of it all. In fact, some days your circumstances feel like they are on top of you. I think that is by design, because it reminds us we don't have all the answers, and we lead ourselves into deep despair when we think we should. David knew that he didn't know, and instead of that making him mad, it made him restful. He was content to trust God with what he didn't know. This, it seems, is a key to great joy, but it isn't an easy thing to implement.

The painful truth of this Psalm is that while it is one of the shortest to read, it is one that takes the longest to properly implement.

I am learning it even today. I hope you are too.

I don't know what I don't know, but in God I have access to the One who knows it all. I am at peace with that. How about you?

Prayer:

Father God, I acknowledge there are many things in my life out of my control and beyond my understanding. Teach me to learn to trust you and seek you in the midst of that.

Psalm 132

The Promise Fulfilled

Reading:

Read the entire psalm, and then read the following verses again.

> *⁸ Arise, O LORD, and go to your resting place,*
> *you and the ark of your might.*
> *⁹ Let your priests be clothed with righteousness,*
> *and let your saints shout for joy.*
> *¹⁰ For the sake of your servant David,*
> *do not turn away the face of your anointed one.*
> *Psalm 132:8–10*

Reflection:

Psalm 132 speaks about God keeping His promise to David, that David's offspring would build a dwelling place for God in Jerusalem. The relationship between God and David is beautiful and complex—one of the complex elements being God's refusal to let David build the temple but promising that someone from David's family line would.

What strikes me when I read Psalm 132, though, is the doubly prophetic nature of it. Solomon (David's son) built the temple, but there was another one from the line of David who really fulfilled the promise. Jesus brought the presence of God to Jerusalem in a way no one expected. He created a nation of priests (1 Peter 2:9) and clothed them all in robes of righteousness that they didn't earn (Gal. 3:27). The cry of the Psalmist was that David wouldn't be forsaken, but it was David's offspring who had to be forsaken in order for God's justice to establish a secure resting place for His presence.

I am so grateful there was one greater than David. If our hope lay with human kings, then we would be in big trouble. Our hope lies in the offspring of David, King Jesus, who brought the presence of God not just to the Holy City but to the cities of the world in the lives of His saints. "Let your saints shout for joy!"

Indeed.

Prayer:

Father God, thank you that you are a covenant-keeping God who keeps His promise to establish His presence with His people. Teach me to shout for joy at the thought of it.

Psalm 133

Unified While Not Uniform

Reading:

Read the entire psalm, and then read the following verse again.

> *Behold, how good and pleasant it is*
> *when brothers dwell in unity!*
> *Psalm 133:1*

Reflection:

There are five church buildings within walking distance of the building that Bryanston Bible Church gathers in.

Five! Why?

Well, we are all quite different, and different enough for us to have all found the need to bring our own unique and particular offering to this community.

I had lunch recently with pastors from all of those churches. It was a meaningful time as we celebrated the great things we had seen God do in all of our congregations over the previous year. We were all thankful that Jesus was building His church in our community. There was a real sense of unity, and I think that if an unbeliever stumbled into our lunch, they would have found it quite compelling to see us working together.

I was chatting to the more experienced pastor who was sitting next to me and asked how unity is typically kept among churches. He came up with a brilliant synopsis typical of a man who has seen more and learned more than I have: *In small things, liberty. In big things, unity. In all things, community.*

I have been thinking about it ever since, and it is true and helpful. It is also multi-leveled, so it can be applied to organizational unity as well as individual unity—God has called us to live in both.

In small things, liberty.

What this means is that we should expect people to have slightly different emphases, tastes, and practices to us. It is what makes us so beautifully diverse. I have learned to enjoy the differences in small things in all my friends, while they really used to annoy me. Go on holiday with some mates, and these things will emerge very quickly. Enjoy them, or if you can't, just let them go, as they aren't worth sacrificing relationships over.

In big things, unity.

It is important to know what unites us. For churches, this is the resurrected Jesus who paid for the sins of mankind on the cross. If we keep our conversations primarily about Him, we will be unified. However, if someone in the group doesn't share this big belief, then real, ongoing unity will be difficult. This is why God asks us to not be unequally yoked with unbelievers. He knows we won't be able to keep true unity with someone when we don't share our biggest belief on what gives life its purpose and value.

In all things, community.

This means we were never supposed to journey alone, so we must ensure we don't get isolated. Again, this applies to both an organizational and personal level. Churches often become so focused on their own thing that they forget they have brothers and sisters in the fight. They tend to get stuck in their own mode of practice and become self-righteous about that mode. Individuals need the constant friction of other people to prevent them from getting too stuck in their ways, and becoming convinced that what everyone else does is unreasonable.

It is a beautiful thing when people dwell in unity. I hope we see much more of it. Where are some areas where you are failing to do that? Make some decisions to correct that now.

Prayer:

Father God, teach us all what it means to dwell in unity and genuine community with others. Forgive us for the many ways we walk on our own.

Psalm 134

Boasting in Busyness

Reading:

Read the entire psalm, and then read the following verses again.

> *¹ Come, bless the LORD, all you servants of the LORD,*
> *who stand by night in the house of the LORD!*
> *² Lift up your hands to the holy place*
> *and bless the LORD!*
> *Psalm 134:1–2*

Reflection:

I wrote this meditation from an airport lounge in the few minutes I had before I had to catch a plane on a preaching and training trip. It was a very busy season of ministry, so I had to fit these in whenever and wherever I could. It got me thinking, though. This whole busyness thing that we all so clearly suffer from—I hate it.

In Johannesburg, where I live, busyness seems to be worn as a badge of honor. The busier you are or appear to be, the more value people seem to attach to you. It means that when we have seasons where we aren't that busy, we feel bad about it and find ways to make sure we fill our time, desperately hoping people won't see us as lazy or unimportant because we aren't rushing to something else. Don't get me wrong, I have been genuinely busy, doing important stuff, and I know you have too. But I do think we need to stop every now and then to acknowledge that maybe our busyness hurts us and hurts our faith. In his book *The Contemplative Pastor,* Eugene Peterson makes the remarkable claim that continual busyness is actually vain laziness in the life of God's servant. He says,

> *I am busy because I am vain.* I want to appear important. Significant. What better way than to be busy? The incredible hours, the crowded schedule, and heavy demands on my time are proof to myself—and to all who will notice—that I am important...*I am busy because I am lazy.* I indolently let others decide what I will do instead of resolutely deciding myself.[23]

Psalm 134 is addressed to Levitical priests. Pastors of the day if you will. Men who have been busy doing all sorts of ministry for the people of God, and the Psalmist reminds them to take time to worship after they have been frantically serving the needs of the people. They stand by night in the house of the Lord, but that doesn't mean that they shouldn't carve out time to bless and worship the Lord.

Maybe today you should allow yourself to have a divine interruption in your busyness? Find a quiet corner somewhere and for a minute or so just lift up your hands in praise and acknowledgement of what God has done. I'm not asking you to take a day off, just take a minute. Watch as your heart explodes with gratitude, and watch as your courage grows so that you can tackle all of that busyness with some newfound energy and perspective.

Selah.

Prayer:

Father God, help me to prioritize your praise. Teach me to pause, to slow down, to bless your name.

---

23. Eugene Peterson, *The Contemplative Pastor* (Grand Rapids: William B. Eerdmans Publishing Co., 1989), 18.

Psalm 135

When What You Own, Owns You

Reading:

Read the entire psalm, and then read the following verses again.

> ¹⁵ *The idols of the nations are silver and gold,*
>   *the work of human hands.*
> ¹⁶ *They have mouths, but do not speak;*
>   *they have eyes, but do not see;*
> ¹⁷ *they have ears, but do not hear,*
>   *nor is there any breath in their mouths.*
> ¹⁸ *Those who make them become like them,*
>   *so do all who trust in them.*
>   *Psalm 135:15–18*

Reflection:

The warning against engaging in idol worship occurs frequently in Scripture. God commands His people from the beginning to swerve away from worshipping anything they can make with their hands.

As someone raised in a Western(ish) context, I always felt that these warnings and commands were for other people, people likely to be polytheists or people who had shrines in their homes and statues of other gods. So, I never paid these instructions all that much attention. A couple of times a year, we would go down to an Indian-themed marketplace called the Oriental Plaza to do some bargain hunting, and there I would see idol statues in shop windows. It didn't cross my mind, though, that perhaps the things we were trying to buy, and the money we were using to buy them, could be just as idolatrous as the golden elephants and cows and multi-headed deities we saw.

In Psalm 135, we are reminded that idolatry is about way more than just carved images and small statues. The Psalmist warns that the work of our hands can end up working us. The things we make can end up making us. What we think we control can end up controlling us. The stuff we own can end up owning us. We really do become like the things we worship.

I may not have a statue of Buddha in my home, but I certainly do have a tendency to worship things I can make rather than the One who makes all things. I pray we would be a people who worship the one true God and who continually use the labors of our hands toward that end.

Prayer:

Father God, forgive me for turning my hope and my trust to things rather than keeping my hope in you. Turn me away from idols. Reveal their lifelessness to me. Keep my eyes set always on you.

Psalm 136

Putting God on Trial

Reading:

Read the entire psalm, and then read the following verse again.

> *Give thanks to the God of heaven,*
> *for his steadfast love endures forever.*
> *Psalm 136:26*

Reflection:

We sometimes treat God as if He is on trial and needs to defend His claims. I hate that I do it in my life—and by grace I am learning to do it less—but it is an area of faithlessness in my life that surfaces its ugly head every now and then.

One of His claims I ask Him to defend is that He loves me. It seems so ridiculous, that the God of the universe would love me, or you for that matter. No offense intended, but if we think about it, there isn't a lot in us that makes us particularly lovable, and it would seem to me that God would have plenty of other things to think about and focus energy on rather than waste affections on us. Yet, Scripture tells us again and again that He does love us, and that His love toward us endures, even when we are faithless in response.

Psalm 136 is a song written for the people of Israel to sing at gatherings. The whole idea of the song was to remind people of God's love through recalling tales of His faithfulness to them over the generations.

> He made the world and everything in it—as a sign of His great love.
> He made the heavens and everything in it—as a sign of His great love.
> He liberated His people from the bondage of slavery in Egypt—as a sign of His great love.
> He gave Israel a land so that they could be His covenant people—as a sign of His great love.
> He remembered them when they were really, really low—as a sign of His great love.

Maybe today might be a good day to take a leaf out of the Israelites' book? Maybe instead of looking for all of the new evidence that God might in fact love us, we should be looking back at the macro history of all things, and the micro history of our own lives, and concluding that His steadfast love for us endures forever. As people who live on the other side of the cross of Christ, we really do have something to look back on as evidence of God's great love.

His steadfast love endures forever.

Indeed.

Prayer:

Father God, forgive me for the times I doubt in the steadfast nature of your love toward your people. Teach me to trust you and to rest in the certainty of that love.

Psalm 137

When the Bible Makes You Mad

Reading:

I have to confess that the last couple of verses of Psalm 137 trouble me deeply. I have been dreading having to write a meditation on it. So here we are, and here are the lines that are so difficult to digest.

> *⁸ O daughter of Babylon, doomed to be destroyed,*
> *blessed shall he be who repays you*
> *with what you have done to us!*
> *⁹ Blessed shall he be who takes your little ones*
> *and dashes them against the rock!*
> *Psalm 137:8–9*

Reflection:

Many of the commentators ignore these verses, and others try to pretend it isn't a big deal. But it is. What is going on here? This is a psalm of the exile—Israel had been invaded by Babylonian forces, and the invasion had been brutal. Those who survived were carried off into captivity with very little but the memories of their former land and the vivid images of what the Babylonian forces had done to them.

The writer of this psalm had probably seen atrocities we can't even fathom, for the Babylonians were known for their brutality. He had seen many executed, and many more tortured for days. He had heard of women raped and brutalized, and he had seen children molested and murdered. As he recalled his rage, he sang a song about how he couldn't wait for the day that the same thing would happen to the Babylonians. He was screaming out for revenge. It isn't pretty; in fact, I don't even know if it is godly—but it is there.

So, what do you do with a passage like this? Here are a few thoughts.

1. You separate things in Scripture that are unclear from things that are clear. As a result, this passage doesn't serve as permission to live like this. Jesus clearly teaches us to love and forgive our enemies, to turn the other cheek, and to go the extra mile. It is interesting to consider that Jesus says these things while Israel is again living under a brutal occupying force, that of the Romans.

2. You admit there have been times when you have felt like this, and you praise God that this sentiment is allowed to be recorded. Some time ago, there was a news article in South Africa about a young girl who was molested and tortured to death. Her father, the accused, ran away instead of facing the courts. When I heard that, I wanted to find him and bypass the courts altogether. I have a deep desire for some kind of payback. I know, though, that my form of justice would be as wicked and incomplete as the justice that the Psalmist desired.

3. You remember that God promises that one day real justice will come, and that the wickedness, sorrow, torture, and abuse we have seen in this life will somehow be put to rights. When I read Psalm 137, I look forward to that day with greater fervor and hope.

4. You acknowledge there is a great deal of violence in the gospel, and that God knows what it is like to have His child dashed for the sins of others. This makes us a little less self-righteous when we read the Scriptures. I, for one, become less keen to judge it and more keen to allow it to judge me.

I hope you know it is okay to wrestle honestly with the mysteries of the Scripture. Let us never be people who become too comfortable with passages like this, but let us engage with them through the power of the Spirit, hoping they will change us.

Prayer:

Father, I thank you that vengeance belongs to you and that one day you will bring total justice to the world. Thank you, too, that on that day I will be able to stand with hope because your Son was dashed and destroyed for me.

Psalm 138

What Moves God?

Reading:

Read the entire psalm, and then read the following verse again.

> *For though the LORD is high, he regards the lowly,*
> *but the haughty he knows from afar.*
>
> *Psalm 138:6*

Reflection:

Psalm 138 is a psalm of praise speaking of the many ways God is worthy of worship and far above any men. Even the most powerful kings of the earth will end up on their knees before Him because they amount to very little when confronted with His power and majesty. This creates an obvious gap between God and men, so I am very grateful for and very sobered by verse 6.

God regards the lowly.

This is contrasted with His posture toward the haughty, as he stays far away from them. He moves toward the humble, but stays at a distance from the proud. This sentiment is echoed and repeated by James, who says, "God opposes the proud but gives grace to the humble" (James 4:6).

I also love how Spurgeon speaks of this. About God's posture toward the humble, Spurgeon explains,

> He views them with pleasure, thinks of them with care, listens to their prayers, and protects them from evil. Because they think little of themselves he thinks much of them. They are low in their own esteem, and he makes them high in his esteem.[24]

The flip side of that, of course, is a stern warning to the proud. Spurgeon further states,

> To a Cain's sacrifice, a Pharaoh's promise...and a Pharisee's prayer, the Lord has no respect...Proud men boast loudly of their culture and their freedom of thought, and even dare to criticize their Maker: but he knows them from afar, and will keep them at arm's length in this life, and...in the next.[25]

Where are some areas in your life where you are living as if you don't need God? Remember that He pays regard to those who don't hope in themselves, and keeps a distance for those who have no need.

Own your need. On your knees.

Prayer:

Father God, keep me humble. I know that is a dangerous prayer, but I would rather be laid low and have you close to me than I would be raised high and without you in this world.

---

24. Spurgeon, *The Treasury of David, Volume 3: Part 2*, 246.
25. Ibid.

Psalm 139

Fully Known...Fully Loved

Reading:

Read the entire psalm, and then read the following verses again.

> ¹ O Lord, *you have searched me and known me!*
> ² *You know when I sit down and when I rise up;*
> *you discern my thoughts from afar.*
> ³ *You search out my path and my lying down*
> *and are acquainted with all my ways.*
> ⁴ *Even before a word is on my tongue,*
> *behold, O Lord, you know it altogether.*
> ⁵ *You hem me in, behind and before,*
> *and lay your hand upon me.*
> ⁶ *Such knowledge is too wonderful for me;*
> *it is high; I cannot attain it.*
> *Psalm 139:1–6*

Reflection:

Psalm 139 is one of the finest and most profound pieces of writing in all of Scripture. It is David at his poetic best, and it has been a tonic to my soul for many years.

Spurgeon spoke of it this way: "Like a Pharos, this holy song casts a clear light even to the uttermost parts of the sea, and warns us against that practical atheism which ignores the presence of God, and so makes shipwreck of the soul."[26]

I am sometimes guilty of a "practical atheism" of sorts, as I forget about the sovereignty of God over all things, including the details of my life. You wouldn't think that one would be able to easily forget such a thing, but I still do sometimes. Perhaps I do it because, like David says, the knowledge of a God who knows everything about me yet still loves me is something too incredible for me to understand. I can't get my head around it, so I tend to live with a functional disbelief about what it says.

I mean, it can't be both, can it? He can't both know everything about me and love me, can He? I think we are all probably a little bit terrified at the thought of being fully known. We have secret thoughts, motives, and actions we wouldn't want people to know about.

David insists that God knows us far better than we ever thought. In fact, He handcrafted us in our mother's womb and has seen every detail of our lives ever since. No thought or action in our lives is kept secret from Him, and no circumstance in our lives is surprising to Him. According to David, that is very good news.

> [7] Where shall I go from your Spirit?
>   Or where shall I flee from your presence?
> [8] If I ascend to heaven, you are there!
>   If I make my bed in Sheol, you are there!
> [9] If I take the wings of the morning
>   and dwell in the uttermost parts of the sea,
> [10] even there your hand shall lead me,
>   and your right hand shall hold me.

---

26. Spurgeon, *The Treasury of David, Volume 3: Part 2*, 258.

¹¹ If I say, "Surely the darkness shall cover me,
and the light about me be night,"
¹² even the darkness is not dark to you;
the night is bright as the day,
for darkness is as light with you.

Psalm 139:7–12

This close attention from our Creator means we are never alone, regardless of how difficult our circumstances seem. We are never able to hide from God, even when we feel we have failed Him terribly. He is always close and so we shouldn't hide, and we shouldn't live like practical atheists by despairing in our circumstances.

He is closer than you ever thought. He is more involved than you ever dreamed.

Trust Him with all you have today.

Prayer:

Father God, you know me and you love me. Such knowledge is actually too much for me to get my head around. Give me a heart of faith to believe it and enjoy it. Thank you for your amazing grace.

Psalm 140

Perform or Pray

Reading:

Read the entire psalm, and then read the following verses again.

> *⁹ As for the head of those who surround me,*
>   *let the mischief of their lips overwhelm them!*
> *¹⁰ Let burning coals fall upon them!*
>   *Let them be cast into fire,*
>   *into miry pits, no more to rise!*
> *¹¹ Let not the slanderer be established in the land;*
>   *let evil hunt down the violent man speedily!*
>   *Psalm 140:9–11*

Reflection:

A lot of the psalms of David are written about his enemies. We can find this difficult to digest today, especially considering very few have us have had armed men chase us with the intention of killing us, every day, for years. That was very much David's reality. He spent a lot of his life on the run from men like Saul and Doeg. They were dangerous men who desperately wanted to kill him, so David wasn't just expressing petty grievances or throwing a tantrum because he didn't get his way. He was talking about life and death.

What fascinates me, though, is who he spoke to about it, and how he spoke about it. He took it straight to God. He didn't wait until he had cooled down or had become more civilized. He didn't wait until he had the right theological framing on revenge before he spoke to God. Rather, in his rage he spoke to his Creator straight away, even if his words might have seemed offensive.

The great thing about this kind of intimacy and honesty in prayer is that it changed David. We know from the stories about David that he didn't seek revenge over Saul, and when he had opportunity to take Saul's life, he didn't. We can only conclude that speaking to God was good for him and settled him down.

I think that one of the biggest lessons that the Psalms has to teach us is that we need to be more honest with God in prayer. Don't try to pretty yourself up before you speak to Him.

Angry? Tell Him.

Disappointed? Tell Him why.

Disillusioned? Cry out to Him.

Faithless? Ask for more faith.

Don't perform. Just pray.

Prayer:

In the prayer today, spend some time (don't rush) just telling God where you are, and asking Him to meet you there.

Psalm 141

Mouth Guard

Reading:

Read the entire psalm, and then read the following verses again.

> *Set a guard, O LORD, over my mouth;*
>   *keep watch over the door of my lips!*
> *Psalm 141:3*

Reflection:

I am moderately "undertall" for an average man in my context. Growing up, I was always called "Little Lester" at school, and it became something of my adopted persona. I was the small guy who knew how to defend himself, and most of my defending was done with my mouth. I learned early on that I couldn't do all that much damage with my fists, but I could inflict a lot of pain with my words. It is a weapon I used much too frequently, and it is still a temptation for me to use it today.

The truth is that words are powerful. They have the power to build up and to tear down, so we should approach our words with caution. In Proverbs, we are told that "death and life are in the power of the tongue" (Prov. 18:21), and David seemed to know this when he prayed in Psalm 141. He prayed that God would set a guard over his mouth, that he wouldn't say things that were wicked and brought death and harm. When was the last time we prayed that?

The Scriptures tell us to measure our words carefully. Proverbs tells us,

> Whoever restrains his words has knowledge,
> and he who has a cool spirit is a man of understanding.
> Even a fool who keeps silent is considered wise;
> when he closes his lips, he is deemed intelligent.
> Proverbs 17:27–28

We often pray that our voices will be heard. Maybe sometimes we should pray that our voices would remain silent?

Prayer:

Father God, set a guard over my mouth so that I will be less likely to say things that tear people down, and more likely to say things that build people up. Let me speak words of grace, truth, and kindness over others.

Psalm 142

Mind the Gap

Reading:

Read the entire psalm, and then read the following verses again.

> ¹ *With my voice I cry out to the* Lord*;*
> *with my voice I plead for mercy to the* Lord*.*
> ² *I pour out my complaint before him;*
> *I tell my trouble before him.*
>
> ³ *When my spirit faints within me,*
> *you know my way!*
> *Psalm 142:1–3*

Reflection:

One of the most difficult things about writing a daily reflection from the Psalms is that sometimes the Psalms can be quite repetitive thematically. It can feel like David, in particular, covers a couple of big themes over and over again. When reflecting on his writings, then, one can either try to steer away from the clear repeats, or one can stop and ask why David, inspired by the Holy Spirit, wrote so much on repeat themes. Perhaps there is a learning in the sameness, a reason in the repetition that can teach us something. I think there is.

In Psalm 142, David is complaining, again. We can stand in judgment and condemnation of that, or we can try to understand why so many psalms are full of David's complaints. David had been anointed as king, and he had been promised by God that he would lead Israel into a new season of fruitfulness and prosperity. But when he wrote Psalm 142, he was living in a cave in the desert, fearing every day that something or someone would kill him. The conditions must have been dire and dirty and desperate, so it must have been tough for David to see how God was going to deliver on His word. There was a massive gap between God's promises and David's circumstances, and from where David was sitting it must have looked like the entire thing had been a farce, or even a cruel joke.

David filled the gap between his expectations and his reality with prayer. Now, before I commission you to go off on a divine whine-fest, there are a couple of things worth noting about the way David complains in prayer.

First, he goes straight to God. When we experience the "expectation vs. reality" gap, many of us complain about God, but David complained to God.

Second, he didn't try to package his complaint. David said that he poured out his complaint and told of his troubles. He outlined what the gap looked like, and didn't try to pretty it up. He was brutally honest before God.

Third, while he doubted the plans of God, he never gave in to the temptation to question the character of God. David was discouraged by his circumstances, but throughout the Psalms he took the certainty of God's character to the uncertainty of his circumstances. We often do the opposite, and when we do, we lose hope. David never lost hope, because he never lost faith.

What do you do with the gap between expectation and experience? Complain if you need to, but do it honestly, to God, while holding on to His goodness.

Prayer:

Father God, there are some gaps between my experience and the way I have expected you to work in my life. Help me bring those to you and fill those gaps with trust in who you are. Please help me, Lord.

Psalm 143

Don't Judge Me...No, Seriously, Please Don't Judge Me

Reading:

Read the entire psalm, and then read the following verses again.

> [1] *Hear my prayer, O LORD;*
>   *give ear to my pleas for mercy!*
>   *In your faithfulness answer me, in your righteousness!*
> [2] *Enter not into judgment with your servant,*
>   *for no one living is righteous before you.*
>   Psalm 143:1–2

Reflection:

Psalm 143 is the seventh and last of what are referred to as the Penitential Psalms. The Penitential Psalms are essentially those that include confession and an acknowledgement of wrongdoing.

In this particular lament, David cried out to God for relief from the pursuit of his enemies, but as he did, he became self-aware to the extent that he knew he not only needed relief from his attackers, but he really needed grace from God. For most of the psalm, David outlined the ways in which his enemy had sinned against him, but he was quick to realize that he, too, had sinned a great deal. So, he didn't just need God to be just—because then he would be in trouble—rather, he really needed God to be gracious. David pleaded with God to not judge him, because he knew that there would only be one outcome: he would be found guilty, and, more than that, so would everyone else.

The same is true for me. If I were to stand before God today to give an honest account of my own righteousness, I wouldn't find any favor with God as a judge. I would be guilty as sin, and guilty through sin. Praise God, then, that the standard isn't me, and that God instead chooses to judge me on the work of His Son. Because of that, there is no condemnation for those who are in Christ Jesus (Romans 8), and that is reason for much celebration.

This week, while I will emulate David in crying out to God in honesty and making my requests known before Him, I will also remember to thank Him for the fact that He doesn't judge me according to my sins. That is a big relief.

Prayer:

Father God, no one is righteous before you. No one. Especially not me. Thank you that by your grace you choose to judge me based on the righteousness of your Son and not on the righteousness I can muster. Help me believe that and rest in that.

Psalm 144

Life Is Really Short

Reading:

Read the entire psalm, and then read the following verses again.

> ³ O Lord, what is man that you regard him,
>   or the son of man that you think of him?
> ⁴ Man is like a breath;
>   his days are like a passing shadow.
>   *Psalm 144:3–4*

Reflection:

I love crisp Johannesburg winter mornings. It can feel properly cold in this city, even though our winters are mild by almost any standard. It is a strange cold that gets in your bones in the mornings. I love the crispness of the blue skies, and the way it's accentuated by the dead branches that partially block our view of the heavens. I really love how my breath forms steam that blows away on the wind. My son Daniel loves this more than anything else, and we were late for school quite a few times as he and I stood in the parking lot watching our breaths become visible before us for a moment before they faded away. It is a good thing to be late occasionally because you have been viewing the world through the eyes of a small child.

Every time I do that with Daniel, I think of Psalm 144. In the grand scheme of things, my life is like that vapor that appears for a few seconds and then is gone. In light of eternity, all of my life on this earth is packed into those few moments that my breath is visible, and then it is over. Gone.

If that is true, and you know it is true if you have ever stood at the coffin of someone you loved, how do we reconcile a God who is running the universe and One who would be even vaguely interested in those breath-length lives? Why would God be interested in us, and why would He think of us? Would He?

Jesus told His disciples in Matthew 10 that even though sparrows were sold for a few cents at the market, God knew about each of them. He then went on to say that God knows the number of hairs on our heads, and that we are worth more than many sparrows. So, Jesus seems to believe that God knows us and cares for us deeply.

This is astonishing, and I guess that is what leads to David's question. It is a question that I often have for God. Why would you care about me? Spurgeon wrestled with the same question, and all he could say was, "The Lord thinks much of man, and in connection with redeeming love makes a great figure of him: this can be believed, but it cannot be explained."[27]

I can't explain it, but I do believe it. It says much more about the greatness of God than it does about the significance of me.

Praise God.

Prayer:

Father God, thank you that you consider me, even though my life is nothing more than a passing vapor. Help me to believe that and then to make the most of my limited time.

---

27. Spurgeon, *The Treasury of David, Volume 3: Part 2*, 356.

Psalm 145

Great God and Great Praise

Reading:

Read the entire psalm, and then read the following verses again.

> *Great is the LORD, and greatly to be praised,*
> *and his greatness is unsearchable.*
> Psalm 145:3

Reflection:

I had the privilege of working as a high school English teacher for a few years. It was a high calling that I should have weighed more seriously than I did at the time, an opportunity to shape minds that were forming and to teach young people the beauty and wonder of well-crafted words. Part of the frustration of the job was that it was quite difficult to convince teenagers that Shakespeare's employment of iambic pentameter was a thing of marvel and beauty. In an instant messaging generation, the brilliance of very deliberate wordsmithing can be a lost art. This brings me to Psalm 145.

It is a masterpiece.

In Hebrew, Psalm 145 is an alphabetic acrostic. In other words, each verse begins with a different Hebrew letter in sequence. That takes some skill, and that takes some time. David didn't just spew out whatever popped into his head—he crafted a great song of praise, because God is a great God worthy of such thoughtfulness.

How about us? Does God get great praise from us? Does He get our best, and our most thoughtful, or are we content with whatever we feel at the time?

He is a great God, and greatly to be praised.

Prayer:

Father God, you are a great God. Teach me to praise you greatly. Show me the areas where I offer less than the best in my life and spur me on to greater worship.

Psalm 146

God and Governments

Reading:

Read the entire psalm, and then read the following verses again.

> ³ *Put not your trust in princes,*
>   *in a son of man, in whom there is no salvation.*
> ⁴ *When his breath departs, he returns to the earth;*
>   *on that very day his plans perish.*
> ⁵ *Blessed is he whose help is the God of Jacob,*
>   *whose hope is in the L*ORD *his God,*
> ⁶ *who made heaven and earth,*
>   *the sea, and all that is in them,*
>   *who keeps faith forever;*
>   *Psalm 146:3–6*

Reflection:

I don't have a great understanding of politics, though I do admire those who enter the field hoping to make a genuine, lasting difference for their communities; but it seems to me that political situations around the world are messy. In our own country, we make a national sport out of government criticism, so the failings of the leaders over us are front and center in the minds of most South Africans. But, we are not alone, as nations around the world are confounded by the caliber of their own leadership.

In Psalm 146, the Psalmist warns us of the futility of putting our faith in those who rule over us. He uses a powerful image, explaining that those who lead us will ultimately be buried in the same ground as the people they ruled over. So, our hope shouldn't be in them.

Now, to be clear, Scripture does tell us that we must respect those in authority over us (Rom. 13:1–7), and we must pray for them (1 Tim. 2:1–2). We aren't called into anti-governmental anarchy by any stretch of the imagination, but we also aren't going to establish Eden on earth through the work of a political party—and we shouldn't hope for that.

So, as God's people, let us not despair when leaders fail us. We should pray for them, assist them, do all we can to make ourselves useful and law-abiding citizens. Let us make sure, however, that our ultimate hope doesn't lie in the princes of this world, but only in the eternally reigning King who will govern justly forever. His government won't ever fail.

Come quickly, Lord Jesus.

Prayer:

Father God, forgive us for the ways that we rely on human leaders to bring about the things that only your Kingdom can ultimately establish. Make us useful to our governments, but make us hopeful because of our certainty in your rule and reign.

Psalm 147

Faithful Beats Flashy

Reading:

Read the entire psalm, and then read the following verses again.

> *10 His delight is not in the strength of the horse,*
> *nor his pleasure in the legs of a man,*
> *11 but the LORD takes pleasure in those who fear him,*
> *in those who hope in his steadfast love.*
> Psalm 147:10–11

Reflection:

I have always been slightly insecure. I am moderately under-tall for a South African man, I am not exactly Brad Pittesque in looks or physique, and while I am a fairly capable guy, I don't excel in any of the areas that the world looks to as critical success factors. I am a decent sportsman, but I was never the best at any sport (except when I played in church leagues, but winning there is like kissing your sister: altogether weird, unfulfilling, and rightly frowned upon by the rest of the world). I was decent at academics, but I didn't win any awards or anything. I am fiscally responsible, but I am no Warren Buffett.

When one looks around at who society praises, it can become quite easy to feel like a failure. Magazine covers show us who really matters in the world, and the chances of me getting my face on one of those are pretty low, unless they release an "average guy just living" magazine. I would buy that magazine, by the way.

We praise the exceptional. We worship them. They can do things we cannot do, so we cheer them on and align ourselves to them as fans because we feel like we can attach to their greatness, in a way.

But how does God measure success?

We often worship wrongly because we assume that God thinks like we do, but tucked away in Psalm 147 is some great news about the kind of people that please God. He measures differently than we do. He isn't impressed with physical strength and major earthly achievement. Verse 11 tells us that He takes pleasure—yes, pleasure—in the faithfulness and trust of ordinary people.

Ordinary people who obey God end up pleasing God massively. Ordinary people who believe God when He says He loves them are the superstars of heaven.

He delights in us when we trust Him.

So, today, instead of spending all your time considering how you don't live up to the world's standards of success, why don't you please God by obeying Him and trusting Him? He doesn't seem to care if you are not ripped and loaded, but He is pleased when you listen to Him.

He is much more concerned with your character than He is with your capabilities.

Prayer:

Father God, keep me faithful, and teach me to value that faithfulness more than anything else. Show me those areas where I am not being faithful, and help me return those to you.

Psalm 148

The Meaning of Life

Reading:

Read the entire psalm, and then read the following verses again.

> *¹¹ Kings of the earth and all peoples,*
>   *princes and all rulers of the earth!*
> *¹² Young men and maidens together,*
>   *old men and children!*
> *¹³ Let them praise the name of the LORD,*
>   *for his name alone is exalted;*
>   *his majesty is above earth and heaven.*
>   *Psalm 148:11–13*

Reflection:

As the Psalms near their end, they pick up the pace dramatically and bust out a praise party second to none. Psalm 148 speaks of how everything in the universe exists to praise and glorify God. Stars, planets, animals, plants, fish, landscapes, seas, rocks—all praising their Creator and pointing back to Him. When I spend time in the African bush, this really rings true for me. Creation feels like it is declaring something, like it is trying to tell us something. According to the Psalmist, it is telling us that God is magnificent and worthy of praise.

The Psalmist then turns his attention to people, and he says that we too have a common purpose. Our purpose is the same as creation's purpose—we are designed to praise and honor our Creator. What I love about his explanation of it is that it is a great leveler.

Kings praise. Princes praise. Servants praise. Men praise. Women praise. Old people praise. Children praise.

We are all united in a common purpose. No one is too rich to praise, and no one is too poor to praise. No one is too powerful to praise, and no one is too powerless to praise. How contrary that is to the divisions we place on people in society today! We continually spread the message that only some people matter and only some people are heard. We all matter, and we all have much to praise God for.

Want to know what your purpose is? Praise God.

Prayer:

Father God, teach me to praise you with all that I am and all that I have. You alone are worthy of all praise. I love you, Lord!

Psalm 149

What Makes God Happy

Reading:

Read the entire psalm, and then read the following verses again.

> *⁴ For the LORD takes pleasure in his people;*
> *he adorns the humble with salvation.*
> *⁵ Let the godly exult in glory; let them sing for joy on their beds.*
> Psalm 149:4–5

Reflection:

I sometimes feel like God just barely tolerates me. On good days, when I can remember that Christ's righteousness is gifted to me, I can still think that is a begrudging exchange—like God the Father has to love me because of Jesus, but He doesn't really like me. In my experience as a pastor, I have learned that I am not the only one who feels this way. People really struggle to imagine that God enjoys us.

Yet, that is exactly what Psalm 149 claims. It begins with instructions on worship and how we are to enjoy the presence and holiness of God, but in verse 4 it then states that God takes pleasure in the praises of His people. He enjoys us enjoying Him. What a thought! Like a loving dad enjoys the company of his adoring kids, God enjoys the company of His people. We are part of that number. What grace.

Prayer:

Father God, teach me to find my joy in you, and teach me to believe that you take pleasure in us.

Psalm 150

A Righteous Racket

Reading:

Read the entire psalm, and then read the following verses again.

> [3] *Praise him with trumpet sound;*
> *praise him with lute and harp!*
> [4] *Praise him with tambourine and dance;*
> *praise him with strings and pipe!*
> [5] *Praise him with sounding cymbals;*
> *praise him with loud clashing cymbals!*
> [6] *Let everything that has breath praise the* LORD*!*
> *Praise the* LORD*!*
>
> *Psalm 150:3–6*

Reflection:

Well, this is it. The last psalm. What an incredible collection of writings, and how well they have spurred us on to live more fully for God!

I love the way the Psalms end—with a holy and righteous racket.

The Psalmist is so pumped about the goodness and glory of God that he tells us there is an appropriate response, and that response is praise. Loud and energetic praise.

Multi-instrumental, raucous praise that is filled with enthusiasm, and, horror of horrors...dancing!

I grew up in a fairly stiff and starchy church tradition, and I was taught from a young age that praise to God should be measured and reserved and quiet and responsible. It was all very British, to be honest. But when I read the Psalms, and especially when I read Psalm 150, I see a response to God I don't witness frequently in myself or in our church. For years, I have justified it by saying that we are just a reserved people. But then, when we watch rugby together, or go to concerts together, we all go completely crazy for things that really don't matter at all.

I am determined, after reading Psalm 150, to praise God with a bit more enthusiasm and vigor. We don't have to go nuts in our gatherings, but we do need to respond honestly, faithfully, enthusiastically, and biblically. The biblical response is loud and full of faith, and mine will be, too.

If God is who the Bible says He is, He is worthy of unreserved and unrestrained praise. We should desire to lift the roofs of our hearts and houses with praise to Him.

Praise God!

Prayer:

Father God, teach me to praise you with appropriate levels of zeal, enthusiasm, volume, and expression. I love you, so please teach me to be someone who displays that truth.

Epilogue

You did it! You made it through this wonderful collection of inspired poems. I hope they have stirred your heart toward greater awe, wonder, and reverence. I hope they have led to repentance, joy, prayer, and singing. Above all, I hope you have learned to love the Scriptures and the God they speak of more and more. My prayer for you is that you would press on and continue in your studies of His Word, and in the singing of His greatness.

Selah. Breathe. Then get back in the Word.

Grace and peace,
Ross

Recommended Reading

C. H. Spurgeon, *The Treasury of David.*

Tim Keller, *Songs of Jesus: A Year of Daily Devotions in the Psalms.*

Eugene Peterson, *Answering God: The Psalms as Tools for Prayer.*

Dietrich Bonhoeffer, *Psalms: The Prayer Book of the Bible.*

Charles R. Swindoll, *Living the Psalms: Encouragement for the Daily Grind.*

C. S. Lewis, *Reflections on the Psalms.*